WORDS OF PRAISE

There is a delightful parallel between [Kornhuber and Deecke's] impressively simple experiments and the experiments of Galileo Galilei, who investigated the laws of motion of the universe with metal balls on an inclined plane.

—Sir John C. Eccles, Nobel Laureate, 1963

From the Foreword:

One of the pivotal phenomena relied on by many thinkers in this intellectual dust storm [about freedom of will] is the *readiness potential* or *Bereitschaftspotential*, as its discoverers, Hans Kornhuber and Lüder Deecke, called it back in 1964/65. Over the years, they tried to clarify the issues they had raised, and dissuade others from pursuing some of the wilder interpretations. Their efforts were brought together in a book, published in German in 2007, 2nd edition 2009, and now available in English. . . . [It] should be required reading for anybody interested in what neuroscience has to say about our capacity to make responsible decisions and be captains of our own destiny.

—Daniel C. Dennett, Austin B. Fletcher Professor of Philosophy, Tufts University

I am impressed how a clever idea of running the tape recorder in reverse has provided philosophers with a way of justifying a hypothesis.

—Arnold Starr, professor emeritus, neurology and neurobiology, founding chair of the Department of Neurology, University of California, Irvine

The quintessence of this very informative and generally comprehensible book, witnessing profound humanistic education of the authors, is the following: Freedom of will is not an illusion but rather an evolutionarily acquired behavioral faculty of man, and fundamental to his capability for culture. However, this freedom is only available in degrees and does not come without effort. The book is highly recommended to all philosophers, theologians, natural and life scientists, and interested laymen.

—Dr. Volker Johst in *Naturwissenschaftliche Rundschau,* January 2008

. . . the brain gives man the capability of willing. He can use it for his own benefit or for the welfare of others but he can also use it in a destructive way. This is not predetermined. Predetermined is, however, according to the opinion of the authors, the ability to do something to enhance one's freedom, to form reasonable insights, and to learn a reasonable self-management.

—Ulfried Geuter in *"Bayrischer Rundfunk 2 (Kultur),"* April 12, 2008

The authors oppose the dogma of total determinism; their approach is a free will evolving from brain processing systems as a pre-requisite for the social coexistence of people and for the development of the individual. . . . The authors integrate in their essay a broad range of interdisciplinary knowledge which often results in unexpected connections and new insights that stimulate one's own thinking.

—Christian Fiebach in *Zeitschrift für Klinische Psychologie und Psychotherapie*, March 2008

The book . . . is an absolute must read. The unabridged read of the book with all its argumentation is recommended to anybody interested in the subject. Because—as the authors themselves conclude—freedom of will is not against nature but an acquired ability of reasoned self-leadership. Total determinism contradicts itself. Freedom of will is neither chance nor arbitrariness, but rather the ability for choosing the good. The fact that freedom of will has a physical basis does not disprove it but makes it real.

—Martin G. Petrowsky in *Der literarische Zaunkönig,* January 2009, p. 31

The Will and Its Brain

An Appraisal of Reasoned Free Will

Hans Helmut Kornhuber
and
Lüder Deecke

UNIVERSITY PRESS OF AMERICA,® INC.
Lanham • Boulder • New York • Toronto • Plymouth, UK

This book was originally published in German as *Wille und Gehirn*
by Aisthesis Verlag (Edition Sirius) © 2009.

English translation © 2012 by University Press of America,® Inc.
4501 Forbes Boulevard
Suite 200
Lanham, Maryland 20706
UPA Acquisitions Department (301) 459-3366

10 Thornbury Road
Plymouth PL6 7PP
United Kingdom

All rights reserved

British Library Cataloging in Publication Information Available

Library of Congress Control Number: 2012931689
ISBN: 978-0-7618-5856-0 (clothbound)
ISBN: 978-0-7618-5862-1 (paperback)
eISBN: 978-0-7618-5857-7

Cover image depicts the Bereitschaftspotential (readiness potential) preceding voluntary movement, as discovered by Hans Helmut Kornhuber and Lüder Deecke, 1964–1965.

Contents

List of Figures	vii
Key Words	ix
Foreword	xi
Preface	xiii
Preface to the German Edition	xv
Introduction—What Is the Will?	1
1 The Will—History and Transcultural Aspects	5
2 The Will—Its Association with Freedom	10
3 The Will and Psychiatry/Psychology	13
4 The Will and Neurophysiology/Brain Research	17
5 The Will and New Psychology Schools	24
6 The Will and the Real Function of the Frontal Lobe—Commander, Delegator, Supervisor and Rater	29
7 The Will and the Evolution of Man—Creativeness and Cooperation—Common Will	40
8 The Will and Dream Sleep, Feelings, Drives, Meaning-Happiness, Beauty, Love, Empathy and Theory of Mind	45

9	The Will and the Limbic System, the Hypothalamus, the Arousal System, Circadian Rhythm, the Endocrine System, Fatigue and Impetus	50
10	The Will Is Not Strictly Coupled with Consciousness—There Are Conscious and Unconscious Agendas in the Brain and Both Are Important	52
11	The Will—Is It Grounded upon Freedom or upon Total Determinism?	65
12	The Will—Its Freedom Is Not a Priori Granted: We Have to Do Something for It—Actively Increasing Our Degrees of Freedom	76
Summary		79
Bibliography		83
Index		103
Name Index		113

List of Figures

3.1.	Bereitschaftspotential	16
4.1.	Learning Experiment	19
4.2.	Compensation of Horizontal Distortion	20
4.3.	Associative Learning	21
4.4.	Imagining	23
5.1.	Visual Tracking	25
11.1.	Evolution of Association Cortex	67

Key Words

will—volition—motivation—intention—freedom—free will—brain—consciousness—humanity—executive functions—Bereitschaftspotential—frontal lobe—delegation of tasks—limbic system

Foreword

As we learn more about the brain, will our cherished ideas about free will have to be discarded? Or radically revised? The implications for free will of research in neuroscience has been a hot topic recently, and quite eminent neuroscientists, psychologists and philosophers have held forth rather foolishly, creating a serious problem of misdirection in the public arena. One of the pivotal phenomena relied on by many thinkers in this intellectual dust storm is the *readiness potential* or *Bereitschaftspotential*, as its discoverers, Hans Kornhuber and Lüder Deecke, called it back in 1964/65. Over the years, they tried to clarify the issues they had raised, and dissuade others from pursuing some of the wilder interpretations. Their efforts were brought together in a book, published in German in 2007, 2nd edition 2009, and now available in English. Kornhuber was determined to see the book published in English, but didn't live to see the goal accomplished. He died in 2009. But the book is now born, thanks to the strenuous efforts of Deecke, his longtime collaborator, and it should be required reading for anybody interested in what neuroscience has to say about our capacity to make responsible decisions and be captains of our own destiny.

Daniel C. Dennett

Preface

Why is it so important that this book appears in English and, what is more, is published in the United States? There are many reasons, here are three of them:

(1) To tell the full Bereitschaftspotential story. This slow brain potential, which precedes all our voluntary movements and actions, was discovered by the authors (Kornhuber and Deecke, 1964, 1965). We offered the translated term "readiness potential" in our publication, but the "tongue twister" Bereitschaftspotential (BP) was preferred. The Bereitschaftspotential can be found in the list of German words in the English language. It had quite an impact; it revived the opinion about will and volition and also about freedom as opposed to total determinism.

(2) A further discovery is that we have shown experimentally that the frontal lobes are initiating and steering a movement or particular task we perform. But the frontal lobe does not execute the task. It *delegates* the execution of the task to the expert systems in the brain, mostly to the motor-cortex-basal-ganglia-loop, but in case of visually-guided tracking movements even to the visual cortex itself. The reader of the book will get at least an idea, a feeling, what the human frontal lobes are and what they are doing. As we expound in our book, there is one important statement: *The frontal cortex is the seat of the will.* This is by no means widely recognized, and the main route of argumentation—what happens when the frontal cortex is destroyed?—is almost forgotten. That is to say, it is essential to incorporate the numerous classical *lesion studies* in our argumentation. By careful studies of frontal lesions in patients we can learn what the normal functions of the frontal cortex are. This is all classical heritage of Clinical Neurology. It was the discipline of Clinical Neurology that collected the largest body of experience about the abilities of man and his brain. This experience had led to two theories (models) of how the brain functions: (a) a *hierarchical* system of centers ordered side

by side or on top of each other, and (b) a *distributed* system, in which, by nerve fibers, most of the brain is connected with many other centers, and this system achieves its performances always by distributed cooperation. The two models were heavily debated over decades. But this was on an either-or-basis: "Localisationists" fought against "network advocates." As the reader will see in the book, we now teach that *both* principles are realized in higher brains.

(3) What then is will? As the present authors conceive it, will is a complex function, beginning with consideration, planning and thereafter, decision, all this taking place in the bright light of consciousness and with self-critical connection to reality, then shifting parts of the processing into unconscious routines but with accompanying supervision, surveillance, control and, if necessary, *correction* until the goal is reached.

We hope that our book may fall on fertile ground: There is a tradition also in the United States, where a movement against total determinism began, promoted by Edward Deci, Frederick Kanfer and others, which revived the tradition of William James, and also by Wayne Hershberger 1989. Deci and Kanfer's key words are *self-regulation, self-determinism* and even *self-management,* terms implying free will. In philosophy too, a new discussion on the will and its freedom began. A book written by Sir Karl Popper and Sir John Eccles discussed the Bereitschaftspotential and Kornhuber's ideas, and in the *"Oxford Handbook of Free Will"* the discovery of the Bereitschaftspotential is also discussed (Kane 2002). In the United States it is in particular the philosopher Daniel Dennett, who is writing important books and is an eminent promoter of will evolving in freedom.

The reader will find all this in the present book "The Will and its Brain," he also may consult its index. In the end, he or she may agree with the authors in saying that it is extremely necessary to counteract the dogma of total determinism i. e. that we are totally determined in all our actions and doings. This would have the consequence that we are not responsible for what we are doing. Such an all too easy exculpation (*"te absolvo"*), some call it "self-corruption" is what people and the media may like to hear. However, it is not so. We do have freedom, inner freedom. Thus, we have responsibility for our deeds, and we can put a veto to bad intentions, e.g. when pursuing unethical goals.

Hans Helmut Kornhuber, Ulm
Lüder Deecke, Vienna

Preface to the German Edition

The term will and related terms such as self-control, intention, volition, etc., totally disappeared from psychological literature between 1945 and 1965. Moreover, until 1965, neurophysiology also investigated man as a passive system only. The investigators applied sensory stimuli and recorded the thus derived brain potentials evoked. Since 1964, the authors of this book have searched for signs of active will in the brain and have found the Bereitschaftspotential (readiness potential) as well as the activity in the frontal brain connected with a learning effort and the delegation of tasks to other areas of the brain. These discoveries were received with great interest by science and philosophy and encouraged psychologists to investigate the will once again. The number of publications dealing with this topic increased and towards the end of the 20th century educationalists and jurists emphasized the importance of the formation of the will ("Willensbildung") for education and the social coherence of society, as well as for the ability to be educated and to work in teams, and crime prevention.

In this time of better insight, however, neurobiologists put forward the theory of an absence of free-will and the non-responsibility of man. Surprisingly, some sensationalist media took up these claims which challenged us to write this book as these voices are erroneous, their arguments untenable. Indeed, we need more rather than less awareness of responsibility for our deeds if we want to face the problems that lie ahead of us.

Our discoveries did not come by chance; we searched actively for signs of the will in the brain. The elder of us (HHK), knew from experience during a long period as prisoner of war, the importance of freedom and will. He has published and, since 1961, lectured on it, which introduced Lüder Deecke (LD) to this topic. Contrary to his teachers Karl Jaspers and Kurt Schneider, both of whom believed in the freedom of will but, as Kantians, thought it could not be recognized, HHK saw that this freedom has natural roots and thus one can help men to become freer — at least regarding the prerequisites for *reasoned* will. For instance, we help to free patients from depression or paranoia through drugs; we prevent, if necessary, oligophrenia (cretinism) by substituting thyroid hormones in the newborn. We try to prevent strokes resulting in paralysis, aphasia and dementia by treating hypertension, and we encourage the capability of freedom through education and training towards an ethical way of life.

The experimental data in the present book were elaborated by both of us, since in 1964 LD became a doctoral student of HHK in Freiburg and later his resident and senior resident in Ulm. LD continued his career as full professor of neurology in Vienna. The author of the text is HHK.

We think on this occasion with great appreciation of the great neuropsychologists of will, Karl Kleist, the great psychopathologists Karl Jaspers and Kurt Schneider, the ingenious cyberneticists Erich von Holst and Karl Steinbuch, of the creative discoverer of the differential amplifier *("Gegentaktverstärker")* and constructor of the EEG apparatus, Jan Friedrich Tönnies, we think of the outstanding Freiburgian neurologist Richard Jung, our thoughts go to our friends the eminent neurophysiologists John C. Eccles, Otto Creutzfeldt, Vernon B. Mountcastle, Ainsly Iggo and to the psychotherapist Viktor E. Frankl as well as to our co-workers Peter Scheid, John M. Fredrickson, Peter Potthoff, Hans-Peter Richter, Doris Bechinger, Jürgen Aschoff, Bastian Conrad, Wolfgang Becker, Jin-Soo Kim, Bernhard Widder, Claus W. Wallesch, Berta Grözinger, Ottomar Hoehne, Katsuhiko Iwase, Tamio Kamei, Rumyana Kristeva, Rosl Riebler, Jürgen Kriebel, Anselm, Johannes and Malte Kornhuber, Michael and Wilfried Lang, Herbert Schreiber, Klaus Peter Westphal, Reinhart Jürgens, Volker Diekmann, Karl A. Renner, Paul Jürgen Hülser, Alexandra von Kirchbach-Henneberg, Erich Mauch, Bernhard Kleiser, Frank Uhl sowie Susanne Asenbaum, Christoph Baumgartner, Roland Beisteiner, Jürgen Boschert, Ross Cunnington, Douglas Cheyne, Rong Qing Cui, Walter Endl, Marion Engel, Markus Erdler, Willibald Gerschlager, Georg Goldenberg, Mary Lee Huckabee, Wolfgang Lalouschek, Gerald Lindinger, Dagmar Mayer, Ewald Moser, Bernd Oldenkott, Ivo Podreka, Alexandra Rutschmann, Josef Spatt, Arnold Starr, Jiri Vrba, Peter Walla, Hal Weinberg, Gerald Wiest and Christian Windischberger.

Ulm and Vienna, June 2007
Hans Helmut Kornhuber
Lüder Deecke

Introduction

What Is the Will?

More and more wars, atomic bombs, genocide, almost a thousand-billion dollars of annual military expenses, diseases such as AIDS, global change in climate, the destruction of the primordial forests, corruption, millions of children starving to death every year, and on the other side, culture, the arts, law, great knowledge, mercy and the curing of diseases through research: Will is an immense topic. Will practically determines what kind of human beings we are. **Man's will** has become the **fate of the earth**, nevertheless, will has been segregated and is still rendered unimportant. Human freedom is the biggest problem of philosophy, the center of freedom, however, is will: For instance, if we become blind or lose speech, we can compensate these handicaps, at least partially, as long as our will is intact. Over all, however, there is no ethical action without will. Because of the freedom problem connected with it, many people negate will. This problem, however, can be approached by research.

If one searches for the basis of will in the brain, a definition, a term, an **understanding of will**, is necessary. Irritated by Freudism, one usually has no clear idea of will anymore, at most a wrong one, that is associated with drive, stubbornness, arrogance, or even with power and violence; this is a subhuman term of will. Will is **reasonable self-leadership of man**, is **thinking and acting out of the personality**, primarily from its core, the self, and from responsible liaison with other people, for man is a cultural being. He is, although belonging biologically to the animal kingdom, a unique being with creativeness, with long term planning, with long-lasting responsibility, capable of innovative problem solving, he is the creator of cultures, whose grand documents from app. 40,000 years ago have been handed down to us (cave paintings, sculptures of animals etc.).

Cultures are clearly not just automatic consequences of brain evolution, but rather the results of a long cooperation of people. Cultures create new systems, which life did not know before and engender knowledge of the world and of man. They even shape new ways of inheritance of acquired qualities through language, through images and in writing, and they enhance immensely the creativeness of life (which is for instance countable from the rate of important scientific innovations, e.g. cf. Lenski 1970).

The **origins of will** date back to before the cultures, they presumably lie in social hunting (Campbell 1970); with this, every individual depends on the reliability of the others—thus social hunting works for the selection of self-discipline, a quality less marked in apes than man. But the beginning culture, with the help of speech, obviously forwarded this development. Culture and will mutually stimulated and imprinted one another, since culture is disciplined cooperation, which is founded on will among other things. Max Weber wrote: Culture rests on value decisions *("Wertentscheidungen")*; we are beings of culture, since we have been equipped with will, in order to give sense to the world.

Will is a complex, **comprehensive brain function**; a narrow term would miss large parts. Comprehensive terms such as consciousness, intelligence, will are by no means empty, we need them in spite of their many aspects. Standing immediately prior to the decision, already driven by will, but reflecting and perhaps inner struggles and then insight; after the planning and the decision there is—despite the delegation of many details to subprograms which were overlearned and then became unconscious again—purposeful vigilance, care, thoroughness, corrections, will of completion and new plans: all this belongs to will. The crucial final hurdle is the **decision**. Power of decision above all belongs to will, but stamina is also important. Prior to all this there is already openness to the world, active searching, perceiving, considering and thinking, the manifold mental interests which already begin in infants when collecting leaves or shells.

There are talented people who still do not achieve anything important. Will is different from intelligence; it shows itself in self-initiative and staying power. In terms of the general staff, will manifest itself in **strategy**. The strategist must not remain ignorantly in the shelter, nor must he run with the crowd; he himself has to plan responsibly. In order to do so he must know his strategic position and possibilities. Above all, he must see what's essential and take a decision from a small set of alternatives. With all the audacity of his thinking, however, he must remain carefully realistic. In terms of economy, will is **management.** An executive must recognize the superior coherences between parts, must set goals that make sense, must be able to plan and organize and above all else, he must lead. Economists speak of management by objectives, management by delegation etc. All this will does as well.

Something analogous to leadership is already present in unconscious nature; in life so many genes are effective that leadership is necessary. The geneticists speak of a **hierarchy in gene regulation** and of master control genes. There is also stabilization of approved procedures—analogous to the tenacity of will—e.g. by the doubling of genes so that if a mutation occurs in one which can probe into possible improvements (but mostly leads to deterioration of function), the duplicate remains functioning; and there is an analogy to the communication of people: the horizontal gene transfer from one organism to the other has accelerated biological evolution in a similar way to language having accelerated the cultural one.

Chapter One

The Will

History and Transcultural Aspects

The literary tradition of mental interests began, in Europe, with Hesiod; he postulated **truth**—an impulse still underestimated: Unhindered by the resistance against truth, the spirit of research has even been capable of recognizing in our days that we live in a universe that consists to a great deal of invisible matter. By will to knowledge, since the ancient Greeks, mankind has advanced—but how difficult was it to fight against appearance and dogma, e.g. to impose the heliocentric conception of the world and, perhaps with even more difficulty, oppose the wishful thinking of the crowd: e.g. some propagandists still pretend that alcohol is good for your health, and this is willingly believed.

Long before Hesiod there were cave paintings and rock drawings, there were megalith cultures that carried out astronomy, there was agriculture and the high cultures with many discoveries and the arts, with religion, laws, technology and script. There was Zarathustra, Gilgamesh and a god, who sacrificed his own eye in order to come closer to truth and after Homer, Hesiod and the Seven Wise Men at about 500 BC, **in Ionia** there developed, on the basis of undogmatic worship of nature, **natural sciences and ethics**. At the end of this development of ancient Greece (in Hellenism), as the sum of occidental thinking, the term **humanity** was handed down to us (with Seneca and Cicero, founded on Panaitius). Humanity comprises everything that makes man to be man and which in the "Enlightenment" period was made by Kant a basis of ethics and politics and which now is an element of modern constitutions. If one looks into ancient Greek thinking and searches for the essential, one finds **sophrosyne**, a term that is often translated by thoughtfulness, but literally means will for healthiness. Diels translates it in a famous fragment (No. 208) of Democritus (who was perhaps the most comprehensive thinker of the antique): "The father's self-control is the greatest admonition for the children"; self-control, therefore, is a term of the will, but not raw will, will with ethos—there is no other will. There is also a verb to sophrosyne: sophronein. Heraclitus said (Fragm. 112): "Sophronein is the most important virtue." The Seven Wise Men already reflected over the will, their parole was also sophrosyne. On the temple of Delphi it was written: "Know thyself."

Without **self-criticism** there is no reason and therefore no will either. Xenophanes, the father of criticism of perception, lived to teach self-critical, innovative, constructive thinking. "In the beginning the gods did not at all reveal all things clearly to mortals," he said, "but by searching men in the course of time find them out better" (Fragm. 18, Diels). The great example among the Seven Wise Men was Solon, the father of the democracy of ancient Athens, who disdained to create order by power, who trusted in insight and law and was successful with it—the only one whom Plato accepted as a great statesman. Heraclitus said that people must fight for the law as for the wall. And: It is necessary to follow the common values. Heraclitus, the discoverer of nature (which is not just a thing that goes without saying but is self-organizing growth, driven by energy, Heraclitus's cosmic "fire," who also coined the term "logos" which to him meant both the law of nature and the capability of man to come closer to it by knowledge) was worshipped by the Stoa as the old master of ethics. Among others he had recognized hedonism as a risk specific to man.

Human will is **reasoned, well-considered volition**, according to the teachings of Heraclitus, Democritus, Socrates, Plato, Aristotle (De anima) and the Stoics (Diog. Laert. VII 1). The **internalization of the ethos**, the decisive element in the deepening of will, was not only elaborated by Socrates but before him by the "Seven Wise Men," and Heraclitus and Democritus, who were not merely nature scientists, made the essential steps. Democritus said for instance: "being good is not just not committing an offense but not even wishing to commit one" (Fragm. 62). "Vulgar-minded things you must, even when you are alone, neither say nor do. Learn, however, to be ashamed of yourself much more than of others" (questions 244) and "he who does shameless things must be ashamed above all of himself" (Fragm. 84). This shame in the internalized (non-sexual) sense corresponds to the internalization of the sense of honor towards honesty, which was cultivated by the Germani and the Romans. Honestum is the ethically good in Latin, in English honesty (cf. Reiner 1949). Plato, however, already saw that the will has several components besides reflection also impetus.

From this time comes the wonderful myth of the **decision to the good**, the myth of Heracles at the forked path, reported by Xenophon. In this, the seduction by hedonism emerges, i.e. the exploitation of creativeness by more primitive drives. A similar myth is reported by the evangelists about Jesus, and at this occasion the saying comes: "Man does not live by bread alone." The sagas and epic poems are full of stories about will and its genesis, as are the tragedies, the fairy tales of the brothers Grimm and reports of mountaineering and arctic expeditions. The will for truth is to be found in the deepest poetry of mankind, Oedipus and Hamlet. Without prudent will, there is no **confidence** and also no self-confidence. The ethical community lives from goodwill.

Will is the mover in the whole realm of the soul, as well as in thinking, says Duns Scotus, the most thorough thinker of the **Middle Ages** (like Anselm of Canterbury even earlier). Duns stood on the shoulders of great Franciscan thinkers before him since Bonaventura: Walter of Bruges, John Peckham and above all Petrus Johannis Olivi, who were against the determinism of Aristotle who was misunderstood by the Islamic Arabs. Their arguments were not only, as became commonplace later, ethical and epistemical, they also appealed to the psychological experience of feelings of responsibility, of freeing, of self-criticism, shame, decency, etc. Olivi calls the will a king in the realm of the soul (Stadter 1971). Olivi's king—here a modern misunderstanding needs to be explained—is of course a sovereign with responsibility—responsibility towards others, towards himself and, according to Olivi above all towards God. Reason and good sense are founded in the will, says Olivi. With intellect and mind alone we would be like animals (summa quest. sup. sent.). Upon Franciscan influences also rests the wisdom of freedom of Erasmus of Rotterdam (De libero arbitrio, against Luther's determinism). Thomas Aquinas too, acknowledged the power of will: "Voluntas vult intellectum intelligere" (Sum. theol. I).

Pico della Mirandola in the **Renaissance** (in conjunction with Nicholas of Cusa's recognition of the creativeness of man) saw willpower in the sense of a sculptor: "According to your own will," God says to Adam, "in whose hand I put you, you will define your nature. We have made you, ... in order that you shape yourself with free choice and dignity you may fashion yourself into whatever form you choose. To you is granted the power of degrading yourself into the lower forms of life, the beasts, and to you is granted the power, contained in your free will and judgment, to be reborn into the higher forms, the divine." Descartes (Princ. Philos. I) wrote: There are also inner acts of will, e.g. doubting, negating and pretending.

Will is practical reason or the ability to act according to principles, so taught Immanuel Kant, the greatest thinker of the **Enlightenment** (*"Aufklärung"*), who saw in "good will" what can be termed good without reservation. Kant envisaged will as being creative, as did the Franciscan monks and Pico: "Freedom is creative ability," he noted (No. 7196 in the inheritance *["Nachlass"]* vol. 19 of the academic edition *["Akademie-Ausgabe"]*), and: "The most important observation, man makes of himself is, that he is determined by nature to be himself the originator of his ... own inclinations and skills" (Nr. 7199). Kant also saw, however, that there is malicious will as well. Fichte said it depended on one's striving, what kind of man one was; and willing was the root of the ego and the real character of reason. Hegel taught (*"Philos. des Rechts,"* philosophy of the law), that will had to act and to obtain freedom by labor. He visualized law, morality, lived morals, society, state as the realizing forces of free will. Schelling said: Willing is primordial being; the will is the proper substance of man. Nietzsche wrote: I judge people according to their will. Jaspers emphasized (*"Psychologie der Weltanschauungen,"* Psychology of the conception of the world, no English translation so far) the will for authenticity and later in "On Truth" the fundamental importance of the will for truth. Similar to Jaspers, Albert Schweitzer was thinking; he noted in the Preface for the sixth edition of his *"The Quest of the Historical Jesus"* in 1950 in Lambaréné: "Imperturbable veracity belongs to the essence of real religiousness." According to Rawls (J. Philos. 1957), justice as well in the form of fairness does not work without will.

However, the **Far East** may have had the most important teacher of the will and the most efficient one in world history. It is thanks to him that China and Japan have their efficiency: Kungtse/Confucius saw the will in similar terms as the Stoics, the Franciscan monks and Kant. He taught self-discipline, telling the truth, working activity, stamina and kindness, tamed power of the character, which in itself had effect on the environment. He believed, just as *Plato* did in his seventh letter, that self-education created harmony without violence. "The armed forces of a big country may lose their commander," he said, "but even from a simple man of the people his will cannot be taken away" (Lun-yü IX, 25). A similar effect in the **Near East** Zarathustra had on the formation of the will: the word and the handshake of a Parse are worth more than the vow of anyone else, which holds even today. In the course of intellectual history, will and its freedom was rediscovered repeatedly. Neither the *humanitas* of the Stoics, nor the *caritas* of the Franciscans, nor the discipline of the Japanese, nor the "dare to think!" ("sapere aude!") of the Enlightenment *("Aufklärung")* are imaginable without will.

There has also been another tradition, which is skeptical towards the will as a high-handedness of man, which was based on the **apocalyptic- (eschatological-) deterministic line** of the late Jewish tradition. It began in Christianity with Paulus and via Luther (*"De servo arbitrio"*) has lasted to the presence. This tradition founded itself on experiences of failure, and it referred to supernatural grace. Augustine had his doubts about how under an Almighty God freedom of will should remain imaginable; he made tortuous proposals in order to rescue the responsibility of man without lessening the omnipotence of God. According to Kant, however, Protestant theology rediscovered will. With Kierkegaard the decision is always the center of attention, authenticity as well; his heroes were the strong-willed Presocratics and Socrates. Also Albert Schweitzer, as great a philosopher as a theologian, was a rational philosopher of will ("Out of my life and thought"); he highly estimated the Stoics ("Civilization and Ethics").

The **modern hostility towards the will**, however, stems from a **theologically misunderstood concept of nature**. Nature, Spinoza taught, is supposed to exclude freedom; this had been different with the discoverers of nature, the old Hellenes: they acknowledged freedom with impartiality. The disappearance of the freedom of will with Spinoza becomes clear, if one compares him with his forerunners, Descartes, Bruno and Nicholas of Cusa. Spinoza's concept of nature stemmed, as already seen by Hegel ("Lectures on the History of Philosophy"), in reality from theology (in fact obviously from its apocalyptic-deterministic line). This theologically-inspired, totally deterministic concept of nature also found supporters among the physicists at that time, e.g. Sir Isaac Newton, who wrote a book on the Apocalypse, published in 1733. Not only an abstract thinker, such as Spinoza, who had been raised in the biblical-theological tradition, from which he later distanced himself, had little knowledge of nature, but even a great natural scientist such as Newton had theologically totally deterministic thoughts at that time. The modern supporters of such a narrowed concept of nature, e.g. Freud and his present epigones, did not understand this. The connection of determinism and apocalyptic ideas is intrinsic in **biblical theology** (e.g. the key-word apocalyptic in the handbook "The Bible & Its World" edited by G. Cornfeld, Tel Aviv). Already in Isaiah there are apocalyptic insertions. In Ezekiel there are a number of apocalyptic passages. Especially, the book of Daniel is apocalyptic, the inevitable expectation of the ending of the world evident even in the New Testament, noted by Albert Schweitzer ("The Quest of the Historical Jesus"). Marxism is also apocalyptic, as Karl Löwith has deliberately brought out. Nicolai Hartmann has made clear ("Teleologisches Denken"), that theological determinism is the hardest version of determinism. An Almighty God, who is willing something, is going to achieve his goals. The natural chain of causality, which is highly intermingled with chance, more than Hartmann could guess, is open for higher determination from reasoned will. If one reads Luther's famous script on the unfree will, one feels that Hartmann was right. Johan Huizinga wrote: For Luther "every human cooperation in salvation would be a desecration of God's fame."

Chapter Two

The Will

Its Association with Freedom

Will, however, has been **associated with freedom** since the ancient world, although freedom does not come from will alone. Self-discipline does not arise without one's own effort, without deliberate learning and practicing. **Positive freedom** in Kant's sense (freedom to… in Nietzsche's sense) is not against nature; on the contrary, it is a consequence of nature in the living human brain, with its cooperation, its meta-analyses, its multifold parallel and higher systems of adaptive information processing with self-reflection, understanding of other people, creative thinking, planning, and decision-making, with the possibility of ordering from the top down to the periphery. Real freedom is capability; it is virtue in the sense of the ancient world. Freedom is always relative: a sober man is freer than a drunken man, an adult is freer than an infant, a man is freer than a monkey, but a monkey is freer than a worm (Kornhuber 1984). Man is much more than a speaking ape. An ape does not possess long-term-planning, has no creativeness, no responsibility (except for its own young), reasoning and consequently has only a preliminary stage of will.

Nowadays **self-organization** is taken as an argument against will and freedom. Self-organisation of connections in the brain, however, does not exclude leadership. Leadership in the brain has largely evolved by phylogeny, in part it also developed through culture and education, finally, however, elaborated by one's own personality from childhood on. The causal connection of the drives is revised by the striving of the will towards a final goal, said Nicolai Hartmann, who by the way, contrary to certain opponents, was not an ideologist but an active scientist, an astronomer; he was regarded by great biologists and neurologists of his time as the most important thinker of the presence. Natural philosophers of our days still adhere to the freedom of will, who are all no spiritualists but natural scientists such as Mario Bunge,

Donald M. MacKay, Daniel Dennett and G.H. von Wright, and others because of epistemological reasons.

Such **positive freedom**, a complex ability of our brain combining with the cooperation of people, is also the most important **basis of freedom from** hunger, injustice etc., which we usually mean when talking about (economic, political, legal) freedom (**"negative" freedom** in Kant's sense, freedom from … in Nietzsche's sense, "Zarathustra: On the Way of the Creator") and at present we often erroneously take for the whole freedom, for all these types of freedom are based on human cultural assets.

For our freedom, which is not a secure state but a dynamic process, **we must and can do something**: For example, we sleep when we are too tired to think properly, we search for information if we do not know enough, we avoid drugs in order to protect ourselves against addiction, we treat ourselves with antidepressants, when we suffer from depression, we educate our children because we want them to be capable and honest, and we keep ourselves busy practicing. Economic efficiency and the creation of workplaces have something to do with will.

Max Scheler (1928) saw freedom, above all, in the possibility to resist temptations, to be able to say no: man as an ascetic of life. However, this **concentration** is less than half of freedom. Even a dog can learn not to eat a sausage from the table, but man can educate himself to do so and he can contemplate nature much more deeply, he can set himself goals and can solve problems; in short, he is **creative**. Those who have still experienced, as one of us, the times without antibiotics, antidepressants and medicaments against schizophrenia or arterial hypertension, know how great the gain in freedom is thanks to these drugs—all direct results of willed research. Csikszentmihalyi (1997), who investigated the conditions for creativeness, again and again found will to be the mover of life stories, however, according to American tradition since World War II and perhaps with prudent understatement as well avoids the word will; he calls it psychic energy, self-control, concentration, striving for knowledge, discipline, attention, endurance. Charlotte Bühler, who likewise has surveyed many life stories, speaks of self-determination.

With animals there are **preliminary steps of such freedom**. W.R. Hess, who was awarded the Nobel Prize for his discovery of the cerebral basis of natural drives, was able e.g. to make a cat—by means of electrical stimulation in the hypothalamus—that hungry that it gnawed on a cable, which a cat normally never does: compulsion because of hunger, a sign of reduced freedom. Our freedom of will is, among other things, dependent upon a balanced system of drives and on an intact cortical control (which, for instance, can be restricted by the effect of drugs). We are responsible for making our own provisions in this sense; for instance, not to drink alcohol prior to a car trip. Our law expects from us that we recognize states of reduced freedom and do not give our car key to an intoxicated person. Even a cat has certain grades of freedom in its behavior, and it maintains this freedom among other things by going mouse hunting in time. Our human freedom, however, goes far beyond that of a cat; we are e.g. capable of selecting among remote goals and of expanding our repertoire of motives through our own activities.

Freedom is always in the process of being made and depends very much on effort; it also is constantly under threat. However, freedom is not only emergence, it is also existence, for the acquired skills, knowledge, and the self-imprinting of the character belongs in will's fundamental core. This is a natural view of freedom. Whoever wishes freedom to be in a mind beyond the brain, must ask himself, where this mind takes information from, how it takes effect on the brain (against the laws of nature), and which goals it can have in a world without natural order.

Freedom is not identical with omnipotence in solo effort, nor does it imply total autonomy. No living being is totally autonomous; we all need water and energy, which comes from outside, in the end mostly from the sun. A hungry man cannot replace his energy requirements by mere will. There are elements that belong to freedom right from the beginning: **tools** and **fire**—and later medicinal herbs, operations, medicaments etc.: these are aids to reach freedom, shaped by the creative will by means of cooperation, including medicines that help the brain against delusion, depression, anxiety, obsession, pedophilia, etc. Positive freedom is capability and introduces possibility. One can do something to expand one's freedom, the will induces and steers creativeness. Taking a problem seriously, already, accepting the challenge, creating insight and if necessary getting together or allowing help by others, all these belong to freedom. In Germany for instance a distortion of the population pyramid has occurred, because the challenge through the drop in the birth rate since 1968 has not been taken seriously and disregarded the younger generation's commitment to provide for the older generation in the form of pensions (Kornhuber 1978); now one has problems with social systems that depend on share of the cost, as a consequence of an ever continuing failure over thirty years.

Chapter Three

The Will and Psychiatry/Psychology

The **naturally reasonable term of will** of the ancient world and of the Enlightenment *("Aufklärung")* of the modern age, which has to do with inner freedom and the creative power of man, also governed the **Psychiatry of the 19th century**. "Health of the psyche is that psychic state in which the effects of free will can be exerted without hindrance," wrote Maimon with reference to Socrates and the Stoics as psychotherapists (in Moritz, 1792). Matthey (1816) elaborated a systematology of the disorders of will including items such as "action on impulse," kleptomania etc. Heinroth, in his 1818 textbook *"Disorders of the Soul"* introduced the term weak-willedness or aboulia, with and without depression. Leubuscher listed in his article *"Über Abulie"* (1847) [On Aboulia] a number of disorders of the will. Jaspers, the first great psychopathologist of the 20th century, pointed at consciousness about goals, means and consequences as characteristics of the will (General Psychopathology, 1913). Kurt Schneider ("Clinical Psychopathology," New York, Grune & Stratton, 1959) said: "Will is the possibility to decide between different inner strivings."

Psychology, a discipline of the humanities, connected will with values (Wilhelm Dilthey), and investigated the conflict and the hierarchy of values in mental development (Spranger). For clarification of the term will in psychology, one must, since William James' important contribution, engage in the discussion about **the self**. This term, already important with Leibniz, Kant, Fichte and Kierkegaard, originates from the ancient world, the philosophy of Plato, and Plotinus the term "self" meaning the core area of the personality. The will proper starts from the self (Lindworski, 1923). That the concept of the "self," coming from the philosophical concept of self-awareness, has neurophysiological foundations, is shown by the "alien hand" phenomenon, i.e. the patient makes movements, but experiences them as foreign (Goldberg & Bloom 1990).

Experimental Psychology began professionally with *Wilhelm Wundt*, who founded the first psychological laboratory and who was primarily psychologist of will. He also distinguished will as the selector between the drives. In the experimental tradition, predominantly Narziss Ach has to be named who combined the method of systematic introspection with the measurement of reaction times. Through this, and other tests, he came upon the high effort of will for inhibition, which was necessary to overcome previously learned responses. It was also Ach, who pointed to unconscious components of will as a consequence of cerebral automation. "In no field of psychology is there greater confusion than in the field of will," Ach wrote in 1910. Kurt Lewin (1926) and Rohracher (1932) introduced further methods; Rohracher, for instance, investigated persons, who suppressed their hunger by will-power.

The deeper cause of the confusion Ach wrote about was the discovery by Wallace and Darwin, that the mind of man is the result of **evolution**. Man was now grouped with monkeys and apes as a primate. **Behaviorism** and **Freudism** in the USA drew rather one-sided conclusions from that assumption for the problem of the will. John B. Watson, in his behavioristic manifest of 1913, threw overboard not only will but consciousness as well as subjects of Psychology. His program was restricted to terms like stimulus, reaction and adaptation. In this field, prepared by behaviorism, Freudism had an easy job. Freud negated will and considered the ego a weak link between the drives and the over-ego; he excluded freedom. The belief in the Freudian dogmas (e.g. the "anal character," which, after 1968, advanced to a compulsory examination requirement for medical students) and the use of a brutalized language (e.g. *"Objektbeziehungen"*—object relations) has decreased by now. However, Freud is still regarded as the "discoverer of the unconscious" and of such processes as repression and sublimation which is wrong. Ebbinghaus already said: "What is new with these theories is not true, and what is true is not new." The unconscious was already known to the ancient world, also to Thomas Aquinas, all the more to Leibniz and the Romantic period, in the first place to Carus.

Then came an ambitious, young brain, who—with a brilliant style—left much irritation behind him; Schopenhauer. With him, in reality, there is neither will nor freedom, but he made without giving note of it, a momentous renaming: he renamed drive into "will," and this converted drive is with him something that rules the whole world like with Heraclitus the fire. Will, however, is something which is different from drive. Drives are primitive regulations, such as hunger for energy demand. Nature gave drives already to the fish, that don't possess a neocortex; drives have their origin in the genes and in the vital demand of the organism. Will, on the contrary, is a much higher cortical function, fully developed only with man; it has well-considered reasons, its counselor is sense and reason, it takes responsibility for values and cultural goals although also considering vital demands. Schopenhauer (1918) did not localize the focus of what he calls will into the brain but into the genitals; with this the Freudians followed him. Based on both Carus and Schopenhauer, Eduard von Hartmann wrote his multi-volume work *"The Philosophy of the Unconscious"* which appeared in 1868 and had great influence. Anyway, Freud did never claim to have discovered the unconscious (Zimmer 1986), and as far as the psychodynamics are concerned, Freud, without admitting it, took the essential insights from Nietzsche; compare Freud and the list of psychological discoveries of Nietzsche, given by Jaspers (1936). The reason for Freud's mental conversion from a scientist to a speculator with a hedonistic ideology in the 1890's (this has also been acknowledged by his biographer, Ernest Jones), was his cocaine dependency (Eysenck 1985). From that time on Freud,—instead of developing new research methods in order to test hypotheses—resorted to propaganda.

Freud's doctrine worked since **the end of World War II** not only in the USA but increasingly also in Europe, bringing the research on will to a complete stand-still by 1965, as Heckhausen (1987) demonstrated by means of counting the entries in the psychological abstracts. **Will, volition and related terms disappeared** from the thesaurus of key words of the American Psychological Association. Freudism at that time became a philosophical ideology. The term Freudomarxism was coined for the teachings of the "Frankfurt school," whose head, Max Horkheimer, had let himself be "analyzed." Berrios & Gili (1995) complained about the term will disappearing from psychiatry as well, pointing out that it is indispensable for the understanding of many psychopathological phenomena. As a matter of fact, the term was that indispensable to communication that surrogate terms were used, e.g. attention, and even working memory. In the DSM III of the American Psychiatrists the weak-willed personality came back as an independent personality disorder. By neuropsychologists the surrogate term "executive functions" was now often used in place of will, but this was only a half-step towards the real meaning of will, for "execute" means to carry out, to enforce, to perform, but the will does not only execute, it also leads. The leadership for this way of thinking was the system of drives or (with cognitive psychologists) the intellect.

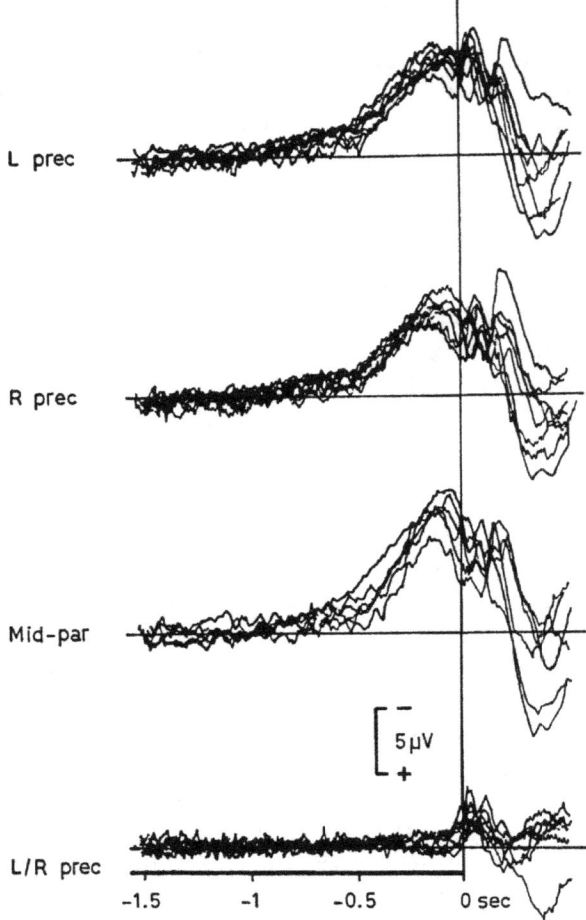

Figure 3.1. Bereitschaftspotential. Bereitschaftspotential (BP), recorded from the scalp preceding willed rapid flexion movements of the right index finger, using the method of reverse averaging. Eight experiments with the same subject (B.L.) were averaged on different days with up to 1000 movements per experiment. Upper three curves: Unipolar recordings with linked ears as reference: L prec = left precentral, C3; R prec = right precentral, C4; Mid-par = mid-parietal, Pz. Bottom curve: L/R prec = left versus right precentral (bipolar recording, difference of the BP in left precentral hand area C3 minus the BP in C4). The Bereitschaftspotential starts roughly 1¼ seconds prior to the onset of the movement, it is bilateral—in its early phase (BP1) it is even bilaterally-symmetrical—and has its maximum over the mid line (Supplementary Motor Area, SMA). From roughly ½ second prior to movement onset there is the beginning of the late BP-component (BP2). It is steeper and now becomes higher on the contralateral side than on the ipsilateral. The Premotor Positivity starts roughly 90 milliseconds prior to onset of movement. The Motor Potential (starting roughly 60 milliseconds prior to movement onset) can only be found in the bipolar recording; it occurs unilaterally at the left precentral hand area as an expression of the discharge of the pyramidal cells of the motor cortex. 0 second (vertical line) = first muscle activity in the electromyogram (EMG). [After Deecke, Grözinger, Kornhuber 1976].

Chapter Four

The Will and Neurophysiology/Brain Research

After the term will disappearing from Psychology, a **new beginning of research on will originated from Neurology**: In the situation of 1964, where man was considered a passive object and only the sensory evoked brain potentials were investigated, the authors of this book searched for signs of self-active will. They developed the method of reverse averaging and found a brain potential preceding voluntary movements (in contrast to passive ones): the **Bereitschaftspotential** (Kornhuber & Deecke 1964, 1965) (Fig. 3.1). It is a slowly beginning brain potential starting about one second prior to a willed movement (e.g. of the index finger). It is a surface-negative electrical potential which is generated by the frontomedial "supplementary motor area" (SMA) and is ten to a hundred times smaller than the spontaneous alpha rhythm of the EEG; this means that it can only be made visible by averaging over many stereotyped movements. The German term was taken over by the Anglo-American language of research (Jahanshahi & Hallet 2003). By means of bipolar recording, one can record the summed action potential of the pyramidal cells of the motor cortex of the hand area, which fire the barrage of impulses via the pyramidal tract (this potential is even smaller). It starts about 60 milliseconds prior to the beginning of the electrical activity in the muscle at the forearm, which starts the brisk movement of the index finger. This rapid small potential of the cortical pyramidal cells (see lower trace in Fig. 3.1) was called motor potential (Deecke, Scheid & Kornhuber 1969). Prior to the firing of the motor cortex, the voluntarily initiated excitation travels through the basal ganglia (Kornhuber 1974), which help the motor cortex to organize the self-initiated movement. With disorders of the basal ganglia (e.g. Parkinson's disease, PD) the spontaneous movements are made difficult, although there is no paresis. The Bereitschaftspotential in PD is reduced over the motor cortex.

The method of reverse averaging to analyze the Bereitschaftspotential was a crucial advance because it made the investigation of the volitional activity of the brain possible. If one employs this method for **learning with the effort of will**, one finds not only the SMA to be activated, but the **whole convexity of the frontal cortex** (Lang et al. 1983) (Fig. 4.1), and this activity correlates with the success in learning. If tracking a moving stimulus with the right hand in a motor learning task and precise tracking is made difficult by superimposition of a slow sine wave (generated by a function generator and added to the feedback signal of the hand movement), which the subject has to compensate by learning, then a lateralization of the increase in brain potential towards the right hemisphere is seen, with a maximum over the frontal cortex (W. Lang et al. 1986) (Fig. 4.2). With hard *verbal*-associative learning, however, the greatest increase of the potential is over the left frontal cortex (M. Lang et al. 1989) (Fig. 4.3).

Thus the prefrontal cortex is not only leading in motor functions but also in **thinking, learning, attending, perceiving** and with the **willed imagination** as a direct test has revealed (Uhl et al. 1990, Fig. 4.4). In this experiment, the subjects presented themselves a slide—by means of a self-initiated button press—which showed them whether they were to imagine a color, a face or a route on a map. Three seconds later, they heard from a voice what color (or face or route) had to be imagined; this was the starting signal for the "fantasy performance." The electrical brain potential first increased over the frontal lobe, thereafter, while the frontal voltage was already decreasing, a sustained potential built up over the occipital, parietal, and temporal areas. The dynamics of the effect of will from the frontal lobe to the posterior cortical areas, which is overlooked by the imaging methods (MRI, PET, etc), is revealed only using the electrical and magnetic methods with their better temporal resolution.

This **leadership of the frontal brain** with subsequent **delegation of tasks to the posterior brain areas** is even more pronounced in Fig. 5.1, which at the same time is an example for the cooperation in the brain and the rapid switching on and off of this giant organ. Apart from what can be called **strategy**, which is localized frontally, there are, of course also **tactics** in the brain. This is the rapid adaptation of actions to the changing situation—without basic revision of the planning. The center for this is in the posterior parietal cortex, where messages from eye, ear and touch converge. In this experiment (Fig. 5.1) the subjects viewed a fixation point straight ahead of them above a screen. They held a light stylus in their right hand, which they lowered to a light plate at a self-determined moment at their own will. As soon as the stylus made contact with the plate, a light point began to move over the screen in a random direction for one second, then abruptly changed direction and moved in another random direction for one second. This stimulus had to be tracked with the stylus on the plate as soon as possible. The two directions were unpredictable, but the length of time (1 second for each trajectory) and

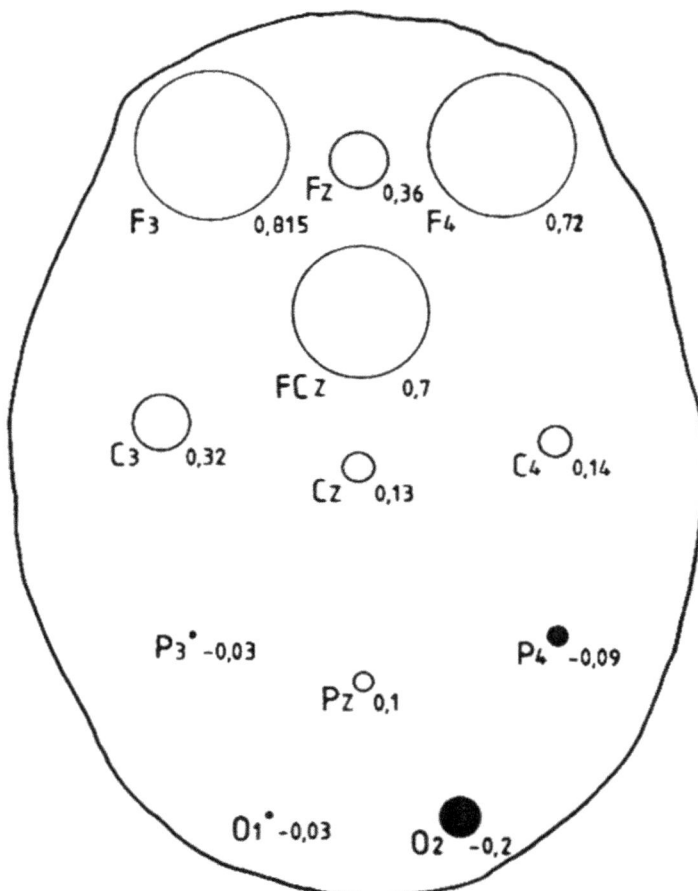

Figure 4.1. Learning Experiment. In this experiment the subjects viewed a screen with a moving light point. Using a light stylus in their right hand they had to track the trajectory of the light point on a photo detector plate. The precision of the tracking performance was fed back to the screen. Using 14 students we investigated, in random order, 3 different types of experiment with 96 sweeps each: (1) simple tracking, (2) inversed tracking (where the movements of the hand were multiplied by -1 for both the horizontal and the vertical component before being coupled back to the screen), and (3) a control experiment, where subjects merely volitionally triggered the stimulus program and watched it without tracking. With the first type of experiment (normal tracking) there was no reduction of the error with tracking; with the second type of experiment (inverted tracking), however, there was a highly significant improvement of performance with learning-effect from the beginning to the end of the single experiments. This learning-effect (reduction of error with performance) was correlated with the cortical DC-amplitudes. As can be seen, there were high and significant correlations over the frontal lobe only (frontolaterally and frontomedially). The effort of the will to track as precisely as possible and to learn from errors is thus accompanied by extra activity of the cortex, the frontal cortex only. The area of the circle is the coefficient of determination d [= r^2], r = correlation coefficient [after Lang, Lang, Kornhuber, Deecke, Kornhuber 1983].

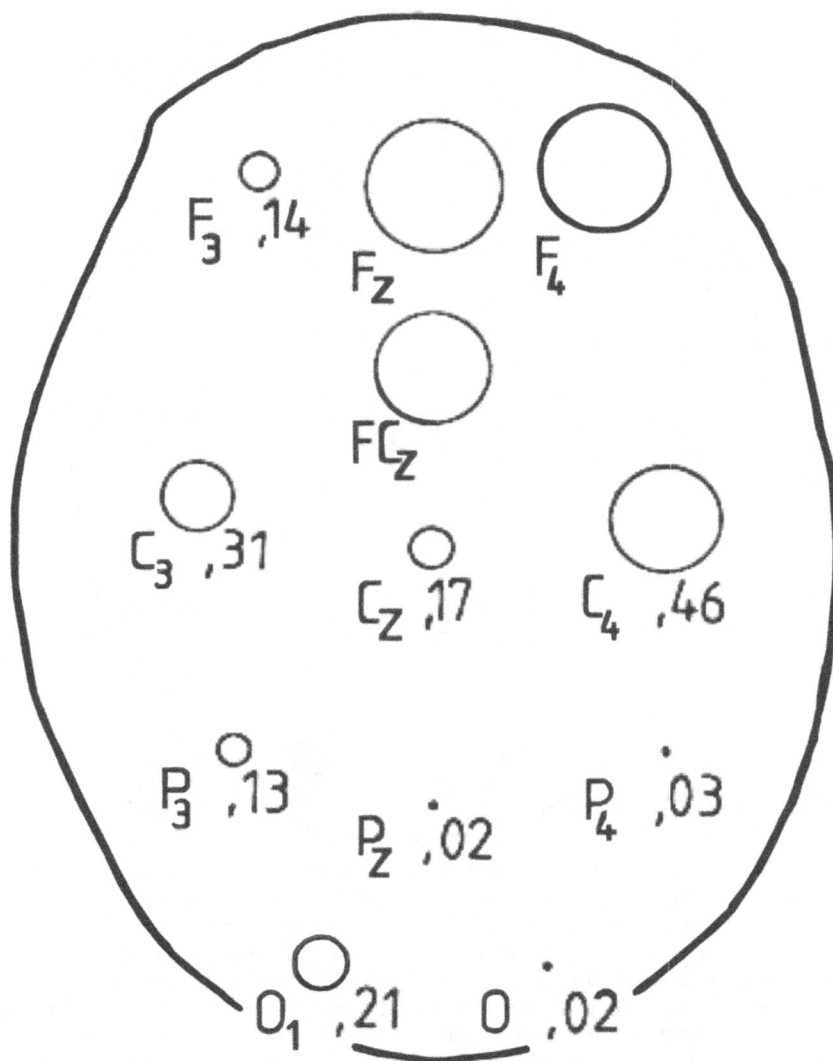

Figure 4.2. Compensation of Horizontal Distortion. In this experiment the horizontal component of the position signal of the tracking movement fed back to the screen, was superimposed by a slow sine wave (half period 4.5 seconds, 20 cm), which caused a unilateral distortion to the right, which had to be compensated by learning. According to the effort of will, there is a lateralization of the learning-related increase in activity in the frontal brain again, but this time over the *right* hemisphere. [After Lang, Lang, Kornhuber, Kornhuber 1986].

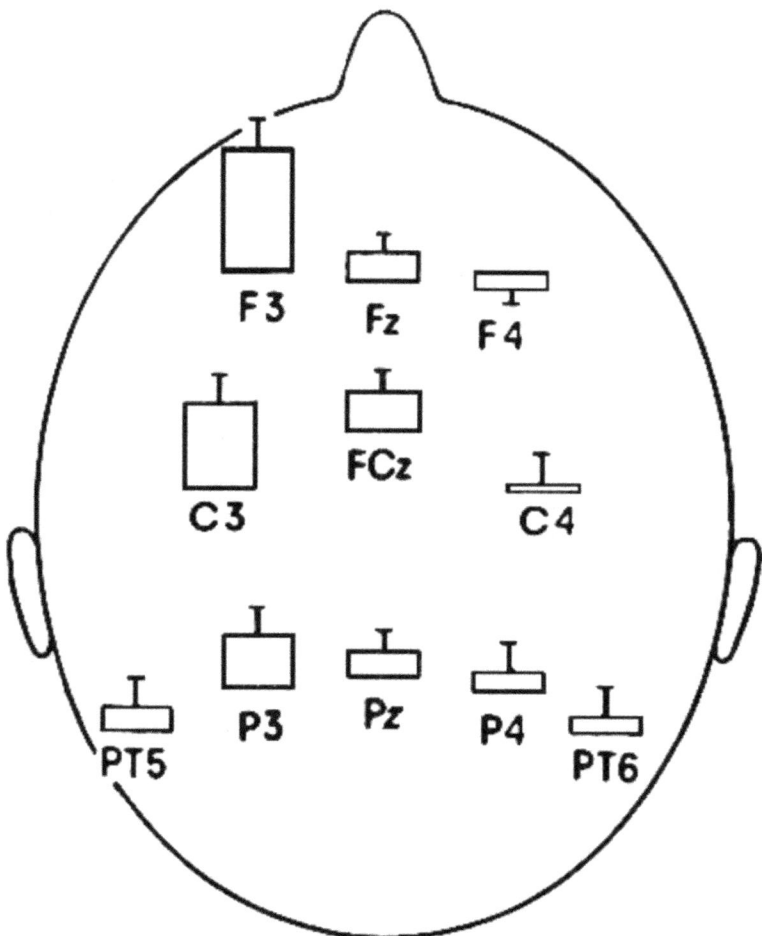

Figure 4.3. Associative Learning. The white bars [with double standard error, 2 SE] are *differences*, which means for each electrode position, the difference in cortical activity is shown between a visual verbal associative learning task minus a control task without learning. Note that the learning-related effort of will produces extra-activities and that these—according to the *verbal* nature of the associative learning task—are localized over the *left* hemisphere and there, fronto-centrally ($p<0.01$) [from Lang, Lang, Uhl & Kornhuber (1989)].

the onsets were known to the subjects. Preceding the voluntary lowering of the stylus onto the plate there appeared, as expected, a Bereitschaftspotential, which had its maximum already shortly before the hand movement as usual, then it decreased rapidly over the frontal brain (here in Fig. 5.1 the recording over the supplementary motor area frontomedially is shown), i.e. "relaxation" in the frontal lobe, while over the parietal and occipital areas (the right occipital recording in Fig. 5.1) there is further activity for 200 milliseconds (this is how long the processing of information for the pursuit movement of the hand lasts). About 450 milliseconds after the start of the trajectory the relaxation in the frontal brain ends and a new potential begins to build up, which anticipates the change of the stimulus: it quickly reaches its maximum over the SMA 300–200 milliseconds prior to the change in direction and then decreases again. The frontal brain knows the course, it behaves in a steering manner through anticipation because it can contribute very little to the elaboration of the direction of the stimulus, it delegates the further task to the experts, the posterior brain regions (Kornhuber 1984). Over the parietal and occipital cortex, however, the potential remains high as long as about 200 milliseconds after the change in direction, i.e. until the job has been done. At the end of the experiment (at second 2 of the recording) the parietal and occipital cortex is no longer engaged but the frontal cortex anticipates the end of the paradigm, maintaining the suspense until the last moment when the stimulus jumps back to the starting point which elicits a final sharp sensory evoked potential. These courses of electrical potentials are so precise, that they roughly match with the 16 subjects, as the grand average of standard error reveals (Deecke et al 1984). Kornhuber saw in these results a support of his theory of **freedom,** put forward since 1961, and now drew consequences in view of the **will,** its prerequisites, its stages, etc. (1973–1995). The discovery of the brain potentials associated with processes of the will, was immediately welcomed in physiology and psychology. The paper of 1965 became a citation classic (*"Current Contents"* 1990). The neurophysiologist Sir John Eccles (Nobel prize 1963) and the psychologist Hans Zeier (ETH Zürich) gave the following judgement of the discovery of the Bereitschaftpotential: "There is a delightful parallel between these impressively simple experiments and the experiments of Galileo Galilei, who investigated the laws of motion of the universe with metal balls on an inclined plane" (p. 152). Kornhuber's teachings of the natural freedom of man were met with approval (e.g. Eccles & Zeier 1980, Zeier 1981). The importance attached by the psychologists around Heckhausen at the Max Planck Institute, to this impetus from brain research, is shown by the symposium "Beyond the Rubicon" (*"Jenseits des Rubikon,"* Heckhausen, Gollwitzer, Weinert 1987).

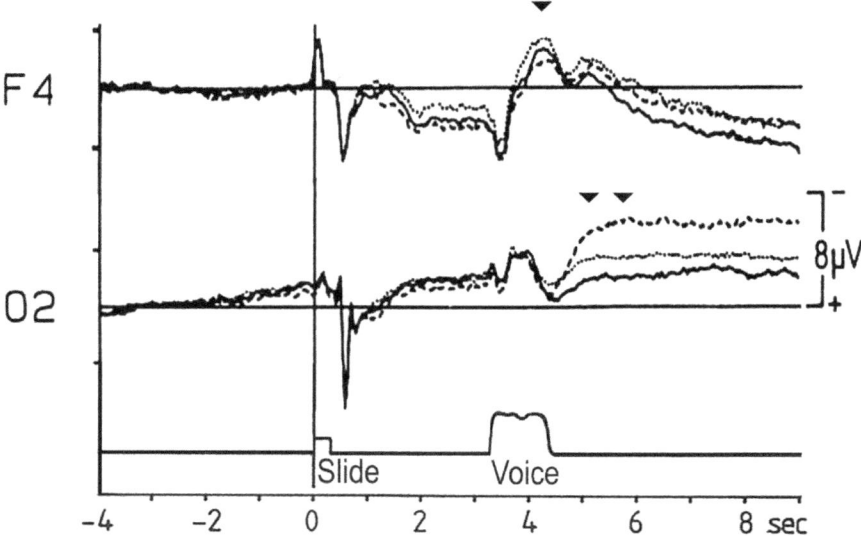

Figure 4.4. Imagining. Experiment concerning imagining ("seeing something in your mind's eye"). Items to be imagined were colors, faces and routes on a map according to the following paradigm: DC potential shifts (upper trace, F4 right frontal; middle trace, O2 right occipital) were recorded from 4 seconds prior through 9 seconds after the volitional initiation of the trial (0 second). The subjects presented themselves a slide by means of a self-initiated button press simultaneously with both index fingers (see time marking 0 "Slide" at the bottom). The slide projection lasted from 0 to 0.2 seconds and told the subject which condition (color, face or route on the map) was about to come. At 3.2 seconds an auditory stimulus started and ended at 4.4 seconds. It consisted of a voice (see "voice" in the figure) that uttered the item to be imagined in the respective category (a certain color, a certain face or e.g. the route from position 1 to 2 on the map). Note that there is a Bereitschaftspotential also occipitally—in view of the visual information on the slide to be expected. Also note that—as soon as it was clear for the subjects what they had to imagine—there was initial activation over the *frontal* brain (F4, upward deflection = activation, see black triangle). Obviously we need the frontal lobe to bring about the effort of will needed for seeing something in our mind's eye. Thereafter, while the frontal excitation was already decreasing, activity built up (see the 2 triangles) over the areas of perception, occipitally (for the colors), inferotemporally (for the faces) and parietally (for the map)—a sustained activation that lasted. This is the expression of the imagination actually taking place in the brain. [Mod. after Uhl, Goldenberg, Lang, Lindinger, Steiner, Deecke 1990].

Chapter Five

The Will and New Psychology Schools

After this impulse from neurophysiology a **new psychological research of will** commenced in Germany promoted predominantly by Julius Kuhl as well as Heinz Heckhausen, Jürgen Beckmann, P. M. Gollwitzer, Thomas Goschke and others (culminating in a symposium of the Max-Planck-Society edited by Heckhausen et al 1987), as well as a volume about motivation and volition of the *"Enzyklopädie der Psychologie"* (Encyclopedia of Psychology) edited by Kuhl & Heckhausen 1996. A similar movement began in the USA as well by Deci, Kanfer and others in restituting the tradition of William James and also by Hershberger 1989, Libet et al. 1999). David Ingvar, a pioneer of cerebral blood flow research, wrote an essay on the will (1994). In philosophy too, a new discussion on the will and its freedom began; a book written by Sir Karl Popper and Sir John Eccles discussed the Bereitschaftspotential and Kornhuber's ideas, and in the *"Oxford Handbook of Free Will"* the discovery of the Bereitschaftspotential is discussed (Kane 2002). Even in empirical social research, where the interest in freedom had disappeared too, freedom was rediscovered (Noelle-Neumann 1978): by means of factor analysis it was shown that the freedom to make decisions in working life was significantly associated with happiness, while the amount of free time and freedom in the sense of "libertinage" did not correlate with happiness and this applied to both blue and white-collar workers. Neurophysiologists, 38 years after the discovery, gathered active researchers in this field in the book *"The Bereitschaftspotential,"* in order to mark the continuing topicality this innovation had and to honor the discoverers (Jahanshahi & Hallett 2002).

The school of Heckhausen and Kuhl confirmed that **will is a complex function**, beginning with consideration, planning and thereafter, decision, all this taking place in the bright light of consciousness and with self-critical connection to reality, then shifting parts of the processing into unconscious

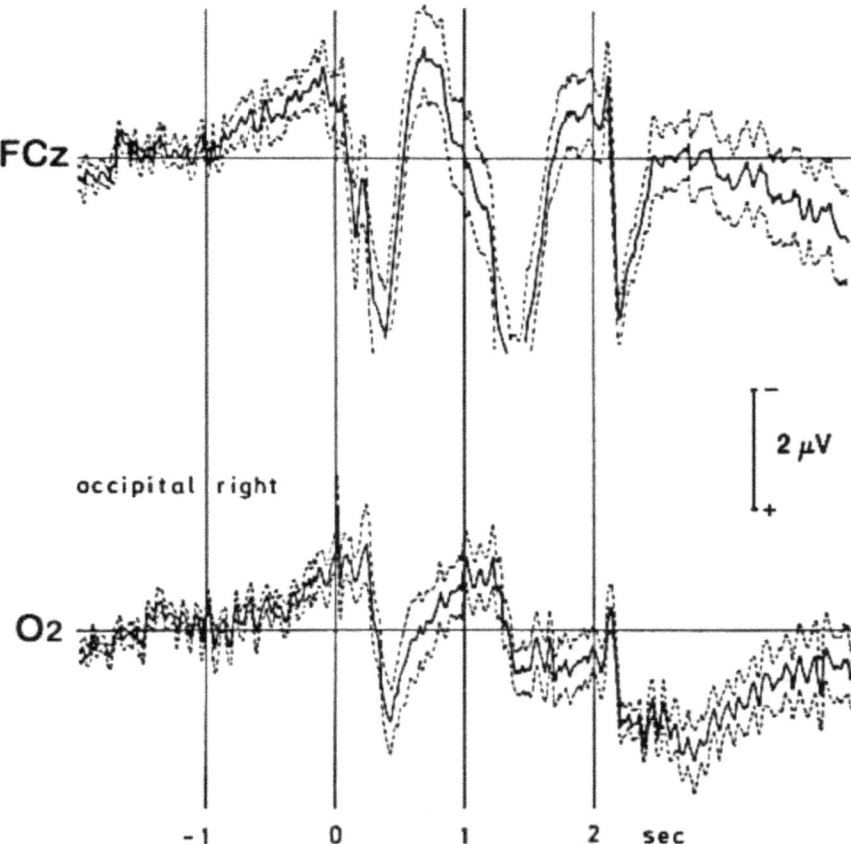

Figure 5.1. Visual Tracking. *Grand Average* of the DC brain potentials of 16 subjects (with double standard error, 2 SE, broken line). Subjects performed visuo-motor tracking similar to Fig. 4.1. They fixed their gaze on a point above a screen. In the right hand they held a light stylus, which they lowered self-initiatedly onto a photo detector plate in a volitional movement. At the same moment (time 0 seconds) a light point started to move on the screen in a first random direction for 1 second, then an abrupt change of the light point occurred into another random direction. The 2 directions were unpredictable but the time instance and duration (1 second) was known to the subjects. They had to track the trajectories of the light point on the screen with the stylus on the plate as soon as possible. Compare the time course of the DC potential at FCz (i.e. over the supplementary motor area, SMA, upper trace) with O2 (right occipital, lower trace): The SMA shows anticipatory behavior in its activation, already ending prior to the light point beginning to move (prior to second 0), while in the right occipital lead, the activation continues across time 0 to 200 milliseconds (*directed attention potential*). The same occurs with the change of direction (at time 1 second): The SMA switches off its activity as much as ½ second earlier than the right occipital region [After Deecke, Heise, Kornhuber, Lang & Lang (1984), and in: Kornhuber (1984)].

routines but with accompanying conscious control and, if necessary, corrections until the goal is reached. After Kornhuber (1984) had already pointed towards different components and states of the process of will, psychological research of will led to a structuring of will into numerous states, which, if we see it correctly, didn't prove very fruitful for education, therapy or the forensic assessment of responsibility. However, it could be shown neuropsychologically by examining patients with brain injuries that the selection of goals and the initiation of actions are distinguishable brain functions (Lengfelder & Gollwitzer 2001). There were also animal experiments with single neuron recordings in the brain of monkeys (Fuster 1973, Rolls 1985) and new ideas came from cybernetics and artificial intelligence (Shallice 1982, Norman & Shallice 1986). An international consensus conference of social researchers, psychiatrists, psychologists, lawyers and neurologists pointed at the urgency of research on will and volition with respect to the prevention of violence (Filley et al. 2001). In philosophy too,—after the neglect in the analytical era—a new reconsideration of will and freedom began (Seebass, 1993, 2007; Nida-Rümelin, 2005). The American Neuropsychiatric Association has now raised alarm because of the neglect of *research on will* and the enormous behavioral problems that occur with disorders of the will (Royall et al. 2002; for a return of will also cf. Haggard, 2008).

All this has not yet had any influence on **personality psychology**. In the textbooks (e.g. Asendorpf or Amelang & Bartussek) the term will does not occur; however, it is hidden in the **"big five" personality traits**, which have been agreed on after 50 years of quarrelling, by means of encyclopedias, questionnaires and factor analysis, above all will is hidden in the factor "conscientiousness." For this the following qualities are considered as characteristic: controlled in the sense of self-control, acting dutifully, planned rather than spontaneous behavior, effective, responsible, reliable, meticulous, practical, cautious, well-considered, aiming for achievement, conscientious—thus all qualities that are characteristic for facets of will but also in the factor, "openness" (what others call "culture," because of the appreciation of arts), which is characterized among others by qualities such as, intellectual curiosity, unusual ideas (fantasy), imagination, adventure, emotion, variety of experience, originally creative—again terms that stand for intellectual aspects of will. Will is also hidden in the factor "extraversion," which is described as action-orientated, full of energy, dominant, enjoying to be with people and adventurous. Furthermore will shines through in the factor "agreeableness," with which, among others, qualities such as helpful, compassionate and co-operative are associated, and all the more finally in the factor "emotional control" (by others in the absence of such emotional self-leadership called "neuroticism"), for which terms such as strength of the ego, stability and self-control stand—all definite qualities of will. It is certainly as Anselm and Duns Scotus saw it: The will is active in all regions of the soul. Factor analysis naturally also has its limitations, and it depends on the terms one has originally permitted for the characterisation of the personality: this was not fortunate for will in the America of the 1930's and 40's when these investigations began.

In accord with this are the basic ideas, discussed in personality psychology of today: there are only two factors: the genom and the environment. It is not considered that there is also **a personality of a child** and **an adolescent**, which first develops perception, motor functions, speech and—through communication—definitions and intellect, but **from the 3rd year of life onwards** the child develops **will** and, thus, **influences its own development**. The problem is obviously packed into the term of "not-shared environmental influences" (not shared with family members), of the non-genetic individuum-specific "environmental influences" i.e. with twins, siblings and adopted children. In these "environmental influences" specific to the individual, the person's own will is naturally inherent, i.e. the young person's personality is also a creative force, the third beside genes and the milieu. The impact of the shared environmental influences in investigations with twins and adopted children upon the "big five" personality traits is smaller than the impact of the "not-shared environmental influences." This is true e.g. for the attitudes and the moral value concepts—even so for body weight. Only with the intelligence quotient are the "shared" environmental factors stronger than the "not-shared" factors. In short, besides the IQ, the "not-shared" environmental influences (and in them is one's own will) are more important for personality than the shared influences (Asendorpf 1999).

A large new **twin study** (Rushton 2004) has confirmed this; the **social sense of responsibility** was determined in 42% by the genom, in 23% by the social environment, but in 35% by the individuum-specific environment (i.e. above all by the people, whose company a person keeps, whom a person chooses for friends.) The largest meta-analysis (51 twin and adoption studies) for causing antisocial behavior, revealed 41% genetic influences, 16% common environment (family) and 43% individual non-genetic factors (Rhee & Waldmann 2002). An investigation of 170 pairs of monozygotic twins and 106 dizygotic twin pairs, even found 50% influence of individual non-genetic factors for antisocial behavior and no influence at all of the genes on altruism (Krueger et al. 2001). One has also investigated genetic influence on the performance in frontal brain tests such as the Wisconsin Card Sorting Test in twins, and the results have been similar as with the sense of responsibility, namely an inheritability of about 40% (Anokhin et al. 2003). However, hidden in the "not-shared (or individuum-specific) environmental influences" is the influence of the developing child's or adolescent's personality itself, above all, the young person's own will. Naturally, important among the "not-shared" environmental influences are also events that happen by chance, such as accidents or diseases, as well as personal friendships and teacher-scholar-relations. However, which personality a child or adolescent selects for a friend or a teacher whom he models himself on or from which books he picks up his ideas, is his own choice, depends on his own will. The fact that will, which can do so much—as the consensus of the Wise Men since Heraclitus and Kungtse saw it—should have no influence on one's own development, is a grotesque conception. Already von Verschuer, a great twin researcher before the era of factor analysis, concluded in 1954 from his investigations over many years that the life of men is formed by factors beyond genes and environment. Charlotte Bühler, who analyzed many life stories, called it self-determination.

His **own ethos** is man's fate, Heraclitus wrote, and Sophocles, Olivi, Cusanus, Pico, Kant and Nietzsche realized that **creative strength** is in it. By means of **self-realization** man reaches an individuality beyond the genetically and environmentally caused differences of animals or plants, therefore the **enormous variance of the individuality in species Homo**. This variation, which follows above all from differences in will and shows up in civil life in a person's life's work (e.g. of artists, researchers, entrepreneurs etc.) but as well in honesty and kindness of simple people, becomes pronounced with persons, when they are under special strain but who otherwise do not particularly distinguish themselves (Kornhuber 1961). It is this variability of people caused by the differences in will and self-development, which makes their cooperation so creative. In ecosystems too, the abundance of species increase their efficiency. Even in the cooperation of the ants there are different "castes." Egalitarianism is hostile to man; the wisdom of liberality rests on a sense for the value of differences. However, artificial variability among people, such as a caste system, which hinders the formation of real differences by the natural development of the personality, is counterproductive. The unobjective stressing of differences, the overemphasis of hierarchy and continuous striving for it, also cause damage. People find inherited differences of economical power often unjustified and unfair, even more so, if this is used in a socially damaging way, therefore the impuls towards communism e.g. with Thomas Morus. Egalitarianism is, however, against human nature, because of creativeness; for this reason communism by force has never worked (a different thing is voluntary poverty as with the Franciscans). The individuality of man, the specialisation and division of labor, has a parallel in the brain functions: in contrast to simpler animals, with man there is a specialisation of the cerebral hemispheres, which help each other.

Chapter Six

The Will and the Real Function of the Frontal Lobe

Commander, Delegator, Supervisor and Rater

Factor analysis puts variety into order, but is no causal analysis. **Brain research** is more profound when dealing with complex brain functions and thus we now turn to this. Will has its substrate in the **frontal brain**, while the centers of the senses and a great part of speech and intelligence are localized in the posterior lobes of the brain, whereby the frontal lobe, being the highest center, leads and steers the action and naturally depends on proposals and cooperation of posterior and deeper parts of the brain, as witnessed e.g. by mood states such as depression. We know the location of the will to be in the frontal brain above all from the sequelae of brain lesions in man; certain preliminary states of will, however, are known from the brain of monkeys, also from brain lesions, fiber connections (Jones & Powell 1970, Nauta 1971, Kawamura 1977, Pandya & Yeterian 1990) and neuronal activity (Fuster 1990, 91, 99; Rolls 1983, 99, 2000, 2002). Since 1965, we have known about the frontal site of the will also from electrical brain potentials and brain magnetic fields in man (Kornhuber & Deecke, Lang et al.) and, in recent years, from imaging methods, especially those (such as functional magnetic resonance imaging) which work with changes in blood flow with certain actions or thinking, train of thought etc., for every activity of nerve cells needs energy and thus increases blood flow, which is taken care of by the brain itself by autoregulation. These methods complement each other: the electrical and magnetic ones have an excellent time resolution but a poorer spatial accuracy, the imaging techniques vice versa.

For a long time the **function of the frontal lobe** was unclear, because unilateral lesions in the frontal lobe are compensated better than the ones of the posterior speech—and sensory regions (compensated by the help of the other hemisphere), and because those specific tests had not been developed which reveal even minor dysfunctions with quantitative analysis. In 1964

Teuber (USA) spoke of a "riddle of frontal lobe function." As a matter of fact, however, the main work of the analysis of sequelae of brain lesions in man had already been fully dealt with in 1934 by Karl Kleist, but his magnificent body of work was not read.

Karl Kleist had shown that the **dysfunctions due to frontal lesions can be divided into two groups**: injuries of the **frontobasal (orbital) Cortex** cause changes in character by the **loss of conscientious behavior**, this includes unreliability, superficiality, disinhibition of desires concerning property and sex, cracking jokes (*"Witzelsucht"*), loss of self-discipline and consideration of long-term consequences, lack of stamina, etc. On the other hand, injuries of the cortex of the **frontal convexity** cause **disorders of mental drive and higher abilities of thinking and acting**. In the frontolateral convexity, Kleist saw the substrate of drive or impetus and active thoughts; in the orbital cortex the substrate of one's convictions, attitude-conducted acting and perseverance, and in the frontomedial cortex he saw the substrate of self-ego and community-ego. Kleist correctly subsumed the two functions of the orbital cortex and the one of the frontal convexity under the term, *"Willens-Ich"* (p. 1170), the will's ego. Kleist was correct in realizing that not only the willed leadership of the movement or act, but also of the thinking, is disrupted by frontal lesions; this was confirmed many times thereafter (e.g. Conway & Fthenaki 2003). The recall of intentions also needs impulses of will from the frontal brain (Leynes 2003). Later on it was found that lesions of the frontomedial cortex too, can cause lack of drive and symptoms of disinhibition; lesions of the neighboring anterior cingulate gyrus can cause **attention-related disorders** and dysfunctions in the perception of feelings. Also the voluntary focussing of attention surely is a function of will. Naturally the frontal brain does not exert its leadership alone, it calls for the knowledge, stored in the posterior lobes of the brain; for this purpose it has its own information system (Petrides 1996). In addition, it takes into account suggestions from the limbic system and the hypothalamus and receives help from programs of the basal ganglia.

The **most severe dysfunctions of will** were seen after bilateral dissection of the masses of fibers that connect the whole frontal lobe with other parts of the brain. After this operation, the **frontal lobotomy**, which temporarily was employed (mostly in the USA) for therapeutic reasons (Freeman & Watts 1942), the most severe changes of personality were seen with lack of drive, complete apathy, and dumbing down of the emotions. A man without language (with global aphasia) remains the same moral personality; a human being without will, however, is altered in the inner core. Frontal lobe syndromes through lesions of subcortical fibers to and from the frontal brain also occur clinically, e.g. as a consequence of vascular insults in the genu of the capsula interna or in the thalamus, and also through demyelination with Multiple Sclerosis.

Oddly enough, these experiences were hardly taken note of, for until a short while ago, in the United States the discussion about the function of the prefrontal cortex was often dominated by the term "**working memory,**" which was introduced by Goldman-Rakic, but was only a renaming of the disturbance of short-term memory discovered by *Jacobsen* in 1935 in monkeys caused by lesions of the frontolateral convexity. This tendency goes so far that one talks of "executive functions in the working memory." Kleist spoke of a dysfunction of practical thinking: it is trivial that one needs a working memory to think. The misinterpretation of the frontal brain function as working memory was explicitly disproved by a direct comparison of patients with frontal as opposed to temporal lesions (Owen et al. 1996): strategy is based in the frontal lobe, whereas, memory-loss is caused by lesions in the hippocampus deep in the temporal lobe.

A further aspect of frontal dysfunction of will and thinking has been elucidated by Shallice in 1982, who, starting out in the initial stages from artificial intelligence, designed a **planning test,** the Tower of London Test, of which now a modification as the Tower of Hanoi Test is also available. Fronto-laterally injured patients have **difficulties in planning** (Shallice 1982, Shallice & Burgess 1991). In planning there are paramount points of view, strategic clearness and practical powers of judgment, all these belong to will. The fact that the functions of drive, planning, and conscience of the frontal lobe are different parts of a whole, as Kleist already saw it, has been confirmed in the meantime (see e.g. Miyake et al. 2000). It was believed that the frontal lobe syndrome could be explained by a disturbance of the temporal order, but this hypothesis has been explicitly disproved: the elaboration of the temporal information is intact; instead we are dealing with a dysfunction of the strategy of thinking (Mangels 1997, Miller 2000). A self rating scale for disorders of will, elaborated by psychologists, has the subjects judge three factors: deciding, planning, and completing (Coolidge & Griego 1995).

In view of the importance of the prefrontal cortex for planning and thinking one would expect that the size of the prefrontal areas correlates with **intelligence** and so it is indeed (Haier et al. 2004). However, because of the distributed, cooperative nature of the brain functions, some parietal and temporal fields also correlate with intelligence; almost all of them are association fields.

There is a working memory in the **temporal lobe** as well, with which we remember e.g. telephone numbers for a short time or remember words while talking, until we have fitted them into the sentence. Structures of the limbic system in the depth of the temporal lobe are also important for the decision, which parts of all the information which flow through our consciousness shall be stored in the **long term memory,** for it would be counterproductive to remember everything. A brain has to be capable of acting quickly, and the larger a memory, the slower and more unreliable the recall. Only the most important information is, therefore stored for longer duration—an approximate estimation revealed that it is about 1% of the information flowing through our consciousness (Kornhuber 1973). Before the evolution of the frontal brain the limbic system decided what was important, and for this reason the basics of the fixation in the long term memory remained in the hippocampus. But surely also the **will** and the frontal brain have influence on the **selection for storage** and on the **recall** from long term memory (Buckner et al. 1999, Fletcher & Henson 2001), for not only the emotionally exciting events can be committed to memory, but we can also engrave our own goals in our mind over long periods, and our will guides our interests, our attention and our thinking, for which we need memory. The prefrontal cortex already influences the formation of the long term memory (Buckner et al. 1999), but even more it takes influence on the retrieval of the memories we need for thinking, for self-criticism, and for the development of the personality (Petrides 1996, Okuda et al. 1998, Thaiss & Petrides 2003). The prefrontal cortex has strategic influence on the memory, on retrieval, storage, precision, care, in case of distraction by similar words, reliability of memorization regarding the sources, etc. (Baldo 2002). Predominantly by bilateral frontal lesions with apathy, the formation of the long term memory is disturbed.

The **long-term memory** is **divided** into (1) the consciousness-prone, declarative long term memory for the system of knowledge and biographical events; necessary for its formation, as explained above, is the cooperation of the hippocampus in the depth of the temporal lobe, but storage occurs in a distributed manner in many places of the cerebral cortex. Above all, the prefrontal cortex is important for reflective thinking about the contents of the long term memory, whereby the basal ganglia help. (2) the non-declarative memory (including our learned skills) does not need consciousness; its traces are in cortex, basal ganglia and cerebellum (further information about memory in Markowitsch 2000 and Poldrack & Gabrieli 1997).

The basis of the **two components** (drive with planning, and morals) **of the will in the frontal brain** (which still collaborate closely) is the **anatomy** (Petrides and Pandya 2002): the **frontal convexity** receives messages mainly from the **sensory systems** that analyze the outer world and whose processed information converges in the posterior parietal lobe, from where messages go to the frontal lobe via long association fibers. The **orbital cortex,** however, receives (besides messages about persons from the inferior visual part of the temporal lobe) information mainly from the **limbic system** and thereby—besides signals from the environmental sphere which warn us about being endangered, from the amygdala and from the inferior part of the temporal lobe—also receives messages from the inner world, about the need of energy, water etc. Naturally, both the fronto-orbital brain and the cortex of the frontal convexity receive the information necessary for their tasks from the long-term memory—information which is distributed across the whole cortex, especially in the association fields. Frontolateral, orbital and mediofrontal areas are connected with each other in many ways and have efferent connections to cortical areas in the posterior lobes of the brain (for the retrieval of information as well as for the delegation of tasks). Furthermore, they have connections to motor (directly via the premotor to the motor cortex and indirectly via the basal ganglia, which are a huge store for programs and subroutines, and thus help the cortex).

The anterior part of the cingulate gyrus, neighboring the medial prefrontal cortex, is functionally a part of the prefrontal leadership system. Relations to the strategy of attention, to the effort for learning and to one's conviction-guided initiatives—so to the self, then—are attributed to it.

The prefrontal cortex, however, has direct efferent connections to the limbic system and to those **deep subcortical aminergic and cholinergic nuclei** that project to the whole cortex and influence alertness, moods, the directing of attention and learning. Acetyl choline e.g. is important for attention and learning; anticholinergic drugs are dampeners for the mind. The frontal brain is that cortical part of the brain, which has the most direct influence on these aminergic and cholinergic nuclei (Gaykema et al. 1991); this underlines its will function. While the whole cortex receives—from the basal nuclei through thin fibers—cholinergic, serotonergic and noradrenergic inflow, the dopaminergic fibers go predominantly to the frontal and cingulate cortex (Arnstein & Robbins 2002). The cortex of will (prefrontal cortex) in turn projecting to the dopaminergic nuclei of the midbrain, receives a positive feedback through this circuit, an inner support and reward for its efforts with learning and productive thinking. Both noradrenalin and serotonin are also important for cortical function, serotonin predominantly for the orbital cortex, which emphasizes the importance of serotonin in depression. Stress, which cannot be mastered, disturbs the frontal lobe function more delicately than the relatively simpler functions of the posterior lobes.

The **basal ganglia** of primates (in contrast to the conditions in birds, in whom the hyperstriatum—the analog of the cortex—is connected only with parts of the striatum) receive afferents from the whole cortex, but their efferent connections go (via the thalamus) almost only to the frontal lobe (including the motor cortex, Wise et al. 1996), which underlines the leading role of the frontal brain. This is mainly coming to action, when new problems have to be solved and paramount leadership is necessary, while the simple routine is carried out by the basal ganglia.

Thanks to its influence on the limbic system, the hypothalamus and the basal nuclei, the frontal brain is in the position to **set priorities among the drives** and **smooth emotions** or else **deepen their proposals with circumspection**. If e.g. erotic movies are shown to volunteer subjects and they are asked to restrain their emotional excitation caused by the movie, activation in certain parts of the frontal cortex occurs that remain inactive without such intention to control (Beauregard et al 2001).

Attention, playing an important role in perception with expectations and presumptions and which, naturally, is also an **auxiliary function of will**, is an example of the **distribution of functions in the brain**, for, of course, the frontal brain does not do everything on its own. When the campaign against the will started, attention was thought to be "harmless," since not suspicious for freedom; attention, thus, was not banned by the Freudists. Even psychologists, who are not Freudians themselves, such as Shallice and Czikszentmihalyi, therefore, use attention as a substitute word for will. The reason why attention appeared to be unsuspicious was that it also has an involuntary, automatic component. Of course, the directed attention, the concentration and focusing with which we follow a stream of experiences and occlude disturbing things, is a component of the will, as such attention with its frontal centers is involved e.g. in the Wisconsin Card Sorting Test (Catafau et al. 1998). The frontal center of attention lies fronto-mesially in the anterior portion of the cingulate gyrus (which is, older by phylogeny, a precursor of the prefrontal cortex, connected to it but did not develop further when the great expansion of the prefrontal brain began), it is the paramount system that takes the proposals from the limbic system and in cooperation with the prefrontal cortex determines the strategy of attention; the more posterior center of attention lies nearer to the senses in posterior parietal areas (Posner & Petersen 1990), it signals news to the front, and it receives tasks delegated by the frontal brain, once relevant actions have been decided on.. Imaging procedures, whose temporal resolution is in the seconds' range, cannot show this **management by delegation**, but electrical and magnetic recordings can, for which we show an example (Fig. 5.1). For the frontoparietal distribution of the attention functions see also Stuss et al. 1999, Burton & Sinclair 2000, Vecera & Rizzo 2003, Birnboim 2003. For the realignment of attention towards new goals, the basal ganglia help the cortex (Meck & Benson 2002).

We will now go through the individual areas of the frontal cortex, in order to make the distribution of functions clearer and the **hierarchical structure of the will in the frontal lobe** (which isn't one way, since there is always feedback for corrections) (cf. Kleist 1934, Stuss & Benson 1984, Malloy & Richardson 1994, Stuss, Alexander et al. 2002, Knight & Stuss 2002, Danek & Göhringer 2005, Gruber, Arendt & von Cramon 2005). Let us begin with the central sulcus, in front of which, as generally known, lies the organ of execution for the will, the **motor cortex** (Brodmann's area 4). When injured there are pareses of the fingers or toes, while arm and leg movements are still possible, as well as a fine-motor disturbance of the tongue and the lips, which, when the patient speaks, reveals itself as dysarthria. Upon dissection of the efferent fibers from the motor cortex, the pyramidal tract, on the level of the medulla oblongata, these pareses remain flaccid forever; the pareses after a stroke in the internal capsule which become spastic are caused by lesions of fibers from further areas; the result of which is disinhibition of support-motor and grip-motor brain stem functions: this is the reason for the extension spasticity of the leg and the flexion-spasticity of the arm.

The **premotor cortex** (area 6) mediates complex volitional actions; with lesions there occurs apraxia. Area 6 receives afferents from the prefrontal cortex and somatosensory and visual messages and it projects to the primary motor cortex, additionally to the basal ganglia and via the pontine nuclei to the cerebellum. The motor and the premotor cortices—as executive organs of the prefrontal brain—can also be regarded as association fields of the somatosensory cortical areas, which are located immediately posterior to the central sulcus: the primary motor cortex (area 4) receives fibers from the primary tactile (somatosensory) cortex (areas 1, 2 and 3), the premotor cortex predominantly from area 5 (anterior parietal region) located posterior to areas 3, 2, and 1.

The motor cortex started to develop with the rodents, whose lips and tongue are strongly cortically represented: these organs need the refined tactile information in order not to be injured by the teeth. With the primates, which need their hands and feet for climbing, fingers and toes are also strongly represented in the motor cortex. Each part of the motor cortex corresponds in size to a similarly strongly developed part of the somatosensory cortex, and only those movements are represented in area 4 that benefit from the tactile afference, thus, eye movements not. For the organisation of the sensory system and the motor system, with which will naturally closely collaborates, see Kornhuber (1978b, 1978c).

The **frontal eye field** (area 8)—which does not belong to the motor cortex and is not supplied by its systemic thalamic nucleus, but rather by the mediodorsal nucleus, which also serves the prefrontal cortex—organizes voluntary gaze. Lesions of the frontal eye field result in a gaze palsy towards the contralateral side, and a disturbance of the gaze from memory as well as searching movements of the eyes in the contralateral visual field; the searching gaze is under the command of the will or of attention, resp.

Injuries to the **frontal speech area (Broca's area)** in the posterior lower part of the lateral prefrontal convexity,—if the lesion is in the left hemisphere with right-handed people—result in a disturbance of the strategy of speech, of sentence construction, called agrammatism. The logical order of speech belongs to the discipline of thinking, and therefore, the frontal speech area lies directly adjacent to the cortex of will. In contrast, for the formation and surveillance of the precision of the phonemes and words, rapid auditory feedback is necessary; therefore, **Wernicke's speech area** is located next to the auditory cortex in the temporal lobe. Thus, the frontal (Broca's) speech area is not the "motor" speech center but rather the strategic one (Kornhuber 1974)—with Broca-lesions sentence construction and prosody are disturbed, the result is an "abrupt telegram style"—and this does not only apply to spoken speech but also to speech comprehension: In order to understand words we need the temporal lobe; to understand sentences we need the frontal lobe (Dronkers et al. 2004), but we need more from the frontal lobe than only Broca's area. The competence of the left frontal cortex for grammar follows suit (Shapiro et al. 2001).

The **dorsolateral prefrontal cortex** and **the frontal pole** (Brodmann's areas 9, 10 and 46) are, together with the adjacent anterior part of the frontomedial cortex, the pushing and planning part of the cortex of will. Injuries cause disturbances of the determination of thinking, learning and doing, of planning, of the production of new ideas (thus of fantasy) and of self-leadership. This reveals itself in the significance of alternative solutions with verbal, motor or figurative tasks, whereby frontally brain-injured patients make mistakes and are noticeable by perseverations, repetitions and infringements of the rules. The Wisconsin Card Sorting Test requires both steadfastness in following the rules and also an ability to modify ideas when the situation changes. Prefrontal lesions of the left hemisphere reduce a person's performance in the Word Fluency Test (Milner 1964), those of the right hemisphere rather in the Five Point Drawing Test (Regard 1991). Another useful frontal test is the random generation of a series of numbers (Spatt & Goldenberg 1993, Brugger et al. 1996) as well as the above-mentioned Planning Test (Tower of London or of Hanoi, resp.) A disturbance of associative learning shows up in tests, in which learning of arbitrary associations is demanded (Petrides 1997); patients with frontolateral lesions have difficulties with this. Further tests that range as frontal lobe tests, are the Contingency Naming Test, the Rey Complex Figure Test (Anderson et al. 2002) and the Trail Making Test (Moll et al. 2002). Increased distractibility, secondary to prefrontal lesions, has also been confirmed in monkeys (Grüninger & Pribram 1969). The "Open Ended Planning" is thought to be particularly sensitive with frontal lesions. It has been investigated with the help of the Six Elements and the Multiple Errands Test of Shallice & Burgess (Garden et al. 2001).

As far as **fantasy** is concerned—it is still underestimated, although in the interplay with directed searching it transforms into what Goethe called *"exakte Phantasie"* (exact fantasy)—it is surely not the frontal brain alone which creates it, but the frontal lobe in cooperation with the posterior association cortex. Will can relax and keep fantasy on a long lead while wandering around memory.

Orbital brain lesions cause disinhibition of social behavior, loss of conscience, disinhibition not just of a hand (as in medial lesions), but of the self-leadership of the personality; they also impair the psychic understanding of other people. This can manifest itself in emotional lability, *Witzelsucht* (joke cracking), sexual infringements, deceitful trading, obtrusive attention-seeking behavior, aggressiveness, confabulation, disinhibited eating (Gourmand-Syndrome, Regard & Landis 1997) and other things. Above all, such patients lack long-term goals and the observation of the long-term consequences of one's own actions. States of uncontrolled **confabulation** (with loss of self-criticism) are, however, not caused by mere orbital lesions, but always show additional severe disturbances in the acquisition of new memory secondary to lesions of further basal brain structures; these patients are disorientated and live in an unreal world; they are incapable of stopping experiences springing up from memory, and they mix them with the presence. The cause is often a rupture of an aneurysm of the anterior communicating artery (Fischer et al. 1995, Schnider 2001). Orbital brain-damaged patients are at times not completely without a conscience, however, they are incapable of transferring their conscience into active will and acting conscientiously, thereby distinguishing themselves from cold-blooded criminals, who have enough will but are experienced in silencing their conscience. A test for the loss of inhibitions is e.g. the Go-/No go test and the Stroop-Test, which, however, demands the subject's attention above all. Orbital brain disorder can be ascertained, better than by tests, by means of examining the history and by observing the patient's behavior (cf. for this Malloy & Richardson 1994). Patients with an orbital brain syndrome are often not prevented from their disinhibited actions by the presence of other people, which fits to the fact that the basomedial prefrontal cortex (besides the frontolateral, *Jacoboni* et al. 2005) contributes to the ability to understand the motives of fellow men. However, orbital brain lesions, even if they are combined with dorsolateral lesions, do not necessarily lead to disinhibited behavior: the over-dependency of such patients is, in suitable family situations, compatible with an active life (Mataro et al. 2001).

The **frontomedial cortex too**, has something to do with the willed control of emotions and with the attention when doing something. With frontomedial lesions, for instance, the drive for collecting may be disinhibited, in this case it comes to a senseless accumulation of useless things (Anderson et al. 2003). The frontomedial cortex, especially the right one, plays an important role with self-criticism for episodic memory (the feeling of knowing). The

supplementary motor area (SMA), which also lies on the medial side of the frontal brain, is important for the preparation and the precise timing of the start of movements (Kornhuber 1984a). The conclusions drawn from the discovery of the Bereitschaftspotential have been confirmed by single neuron recordings from the SMA of man (Amador & Fried 2004), thereby it was found that SMA-neurons behave differently with voluntary movements that are only imagined as opposed to those actually executed. With voluntary movements not preceded by an external stimulus, the **basal ganglia** help the motor cortex by providing the appropriate programmes. The temporal course of this neuronal activity was investigated by Cunnington, Deecke and co-workers (1999, 2002) using functional magnetic tomography: At first, the SMA and the directly adjacent region in the anterior cingulate gyrus are activated, then the basal ganglia (and especially the nucleus lentiformis), and only thereafter the primary motor cortex. Even the Bereitschaftspotential itself can be recorded in the basal ganglia (Rektor et al. 2001, Rektor 2003). The information runs from the basal ganglia via the thalamus back to the cortex (Kornhuber 1974). The SMA takes the initiative and distributes the tasks in space and time. However, the basal ganglia only become active with the self-initiated movements and what is more, they become active *prior* to the start of the movement. The basal ganglia do not become active in the case of movements that are triggered by external stimuli (Cunnington et al. 2002). During this time the Bereitschaftspotential builds up (Fig. 3.1) prior to self-initiated voluntary movement. The supplementary motor area controls, whether the time of the movement and the programs fit. If one asks subjects to perform short series of single movements of the fingers, and stimulates the contralateral primary motor area with repetitive transcranial magnetic stimulation (thereby exerting a transient local turn-off of the cortical function) the series of finger movements is immediately interrupted, because the fingers are paralyzed. However, if the SMA is transiently turned off by brisk repetitive magnetic-disturbing stimuli, the motor cortex finishes the current sequence, but cannot start the next one (Gerloff et al. 1997). Lesions of the left SMA (in right-handed people) also cause a disturbance of speech in particular if the production of articulatory sequences is concerned. The result is a slowed speech with disruptions (Ziegler et al. 1997). With SMA lesions, on the one hand a dysfunction of motor spontaneity to the extent of akinetic mutism can occur; on the other hand disinhibition symptoms of elementary movements of the arm and the hand can appear, **alien hand syndrome**, whereby the hand performs movements that the patient experiences as not willed, as not carried out by himself: this is a dysfunction of the voluntary control of spontaneous impulses of the basal ganglia. Here, in contrast to the orbital lesions, the morals are not disturbed (Scepkowski & Cronin-Golomb 2003).

The **basal ganglia** do groundwork for the motor cortex among others for movements of the extremities and the trunk (Kornhuber 1974, 1977). For example, a patient with athetosis caused by a lesion in the basal ganglia, has no paresis of the arm; he can move his arm and hand which, in a contracted flexion position, persist in a quasi spastic immobility. Still he can move these limbs in both directions, flexion and extension. How does he do this? He "activates" the palm with the other hand by tactile stimuli and like through magnetic force guides the movement in the desired direction. This ("magnetic") effect goes via the somatosensory cortex to the motor cortex. The basal ganglia also help the association cortex, e.g. when speaking (Brunner et al. 1982). Lesions of the basal ganglia, in addition to cortical lesions of Wernicke's area, worsen the aphasia and cause verbal perseverations with the same verbal material uttered again and again: The speech intention keeps erroneously activating the same subroutine. Also verbal tics occur, apart from involuntary movements, as disinhibition symptoms secondary to basal ganglia lesions (Kornhuber 1977). Global aphasia and severe aphasias with primitive perseverations ("recurrent utterances") are usually not caused by lesions of Wernicke's and Broca's speech areas alone, but by combined lesions of Wernicke's area and the basal ganglia. Thus it is no wonder that the part of the brain, which comes next to the enormous evolutionary enlargement of the neocortical association fields (especially the frontal brain of man) are the basal ganglia (Stephan et al. 1988), whereas the limbic system, which is old in phylogeny, remains conservative. Kornhuber's ideas about the role of the basal ganglia as a store for programmes, have been confirmed and described in detail by Wallesch (1990) and Wise et al. (1996). The basal ganglia and their cooperation with the frontal brain also play a role in the genesis of obsessional phenomena and compulsive disorders (Cummings & Frankel 1985, Berthier et al. 2001, Kwon et al. 2003). These dysfunctions, a segmental kind of disturbance of will, can be influenced therapeutically with neuroleptics and new antidepressants (selective serotonin re-uptake inhibitors) as well as with (cognitive) behavior therapy. For neurophysiology of the basal ganglia, see Alexander, DeLong & Strick 1986, as well as Alexander, Crutcher & DeLong 1990.

Chapter Seven

The Will and the Evolution of Man

Creativeness and Cooperation—Common Will

The remarkable feature in the **evolution of man** is not "the drives," for we assume these also in animals (e.g. dogs whose social behavior is particularly close to man, obviously because they are also social hunters), but the **mind**, which then also "humanizes" emotions. In the mental sphere it is not only **speech**—which after the upright gait, was probably already present in *Homo habilis* two million years ago as an early step on the evolutionary way to mankind (Holloway, 1983; Tobias 1987) and which enabled differentiated cooperation—but also the **creativeness** of the frontal lobe and the reasoned will (Kornhuber 1995), because sign language can be learned by young apes, but these subhuman primates cannot themselves generate speech, in contrast to deaf-mute children, who can develop on their own, i.e. without external hints, a sign language for their communication (Goldin-Meadow & Feldman 1977). The apes cannot learn a vocal language because they lack Wernicke's area in the temporal lobe, which lies in the vicinity of the primary auditory area and is necessary for the rapid auditory control of the phonemes, without which language is incomprehensible. Thus, the real motor cortex for speaking is this sensory speech area, not the precentral motor cortex. If this was damaged, aphasias were never observed but only unclear articulation (dysarthria). The frontal speech area (Broca's area) is in charge of the strategy of speech, i.e. the construction of sentences not of the control of single words. The differentiated cooperation of early man—especially with hunting, by means of language e.g. *Homo habilis* two million years ago, who probably already possessed a Wernicke's area (Holloway 1983, Tobias 1987) and was able to speak, although he had only half the brain of *Homo sapiens*—obviously led to the **selection within the species re intelligence and creativeness** and, therefore, to these astonishingly quick advances. The significant result, however, was not just "more speech," it was **creativeness** (Kornhuber

1984, 1993); and with this, man became dangerous to man (especially as he was now tied down less by instincts) and, thus, he needed **human morals**: **conscience and fairness** beyond the care of the brood, and what is more, the closeness and cooperation of creativeness with **moral will** in the frontal lobe of man. Creativeness is by no means only a feature of some artists and inventors in advanced cultures. Every child paints. In the whole of Africa there are millions of rock paintings made by Bushmen. The "steel hard cage of modern bureaucracy" (Max Weber) is a delusion: Man is a cultural being, and culture is crystallized creativeness. Man is—other than Gehlen saw it— the contrary of a "deficiency being"; he has an abundance of creativeness. Of course, will on its own does not achieve creativeness but it elicits it, organises it, and brings it to success, naturally in conjunction with the whole brain and together with other people.

The notion that the essence of man is **creativeness** had already Sophocles in his famous chorus in "Antigone" and then again Pico della Mirandola in his tract on the dignity of man. *Sophocles* also already understood that man's creativeness is not only magnificent but also **dangerous**; he, therefore, called man (with the superlative for *deinos*) *deinotatos*, which is normally translated by enormous or tremendous, but which really means dreadful or terrifying (the word dinosaur is also derived from it). One doesn't have to go as far as the atomic bombs on Hiroshima and Nagasaki to see this, the use of fire or speech can be bad enough. By these two terms man distinguished himself right from the beginning. Since the New Stone Age he has changed the biosphere, and in the 20th century, man has become the main problem of the earth. Man causes the tropical rain-forests to lose one percent of their area per year, and the extinction rate of the flowering plants and the vertebrates is now probably 50 to 100 times above the natural rate.

The reason, why human morals could become a selection factor, lies in the advantages of self-disciplined **cooperation**, which above all else is the reason for the superiority of man. This is a point, the Social Darwinists did not understand, but Solon did, as did Plato and Aristotle, Kungtse, Gautama, Jesus, Hugo Grotius, Montesquieu, Immanuel Kant, Baron vom Stein, Henry Dunant, Raiffeisen, and the Prince Kropotkin, but also Charles Darwin himself in his book "The descent of man" (1871), which is too little observed: With the evolution within a species cooperation is more important than competition. It was not the class-struggle propagandist and admirer of the terror of the Paris commune (which set an example for the terror of Lenin, Trotzki and Stalin) Karl Marx, but rather the cooperative thinker of social order, Lorenz von Stein who suggested those innovations that gave more solidarity to the life of the Europeans: on his ideas rest the social reforms of Bismarck and his counsellors. To elicit cooperation with conviction yet without pressure, is the prime art of leadership, both, within one's soul and interpersonally. To be on bad terms with each other is repulsive, and is frequently the main reason for a political party being voted out of office.

Stabilization of the will through **common will** is achieved by families, orchestras etc. in short, by **communities**. Professor Yunus in Bangladesh (who received the Nobel peace prize for this) has proved that economy is based not only on competition but also on community; he successfully gives credits without additional security to persons (predominantly women), who promise to work together in small groups—a confirmation of the ideas of Ferdinand Tönnies and Kropotkin.

A kind of cooperation can already be observed on the level of physics and chemistry—for example, the strength of the aromatic ring depends on a special cooperation of the atoms in the molecule—however, cooperation is predominantly realized in life: in the eukaryotic cell, the mitochondria, initially independent living things, deliver energy for higher purposes, and the co-evolution of insects and plants has brought us the wonder world of colors and scents of blossoms. Also wonderful is the co-interaction of the genes, which from the same basic elements of information create the variety of living beings and their organs, etc. The same gene, which, in mice and men, steers the development of an eye with lenses, brings about—e.g. in fruit-flies, in cooperation with other genes—the typical insect compound eye (Quiring et al. 1994, Halder et al. 1995). This gene is a master control gene, in charge of the formation of eyes from the sea squirts and cephalopodes via the insects to the vertebrates, but how the individual eye is then constructed, can vary widely. In the brain too, there is cooperation, e.g. of cortical columns, which are principally all similar, (Mountcastle 1957, Powell & Mountcastle 1959): by their cooperation perceptions on the one hand, and thoughts and movements on the other can be generated. The cooperation of people, however, is not fixed as it is with genes by gene regulation or as it is with ants in an ant colony by instincts. People can overcome egoisms and come to cooperation beyond family bonds for the common benefit, for remote goals and ideas. For this, leadership personalities (e.g. Solon or Francis of Assisi) play an important role.

However, **truth** is particularly important for cooperation. For this goal, those who seek the truth and those who steadfastly oppose error and lies are vital: Shining personalities of mankind such as Heraclitus, Socrates, Bruno, Copernicus, Spinoza, Lessing, Wallace and Darwin, Albert Schweitzer. Campaigns of organized propaganda of lies spreading in particularly in conjunction with wars, nationalism, imperialism and economical interests (arms trade, alcohol, cigarettes), have a poisoning effect. The orbitofrontal areas, serving conscience, are phylogenetically the youngest in man (Spatz 1951). Mutual help, including help for handicapped old people, was already realized with *Homo erectus,* 1.7 million years ogo (Lordkipanidze et al. 2005).

Creativeness is tested by its consequences for the world, and aids for testing are the experiences of generations, which are handed down as standards and values. The necessity that **morals have to relate to more than man only**, the occident has only begun to understand—after two and a half millenia of ethical discussion—since Alexander von Humboldt and Albert Schweitzer. *Goethe* taught (in the *"Pedagogical Province"* in *"Wilhelm Meister's Journeyman Years"*) respect also towards "what is below us."

The fact that neither language nor the temporoparietal association cortex are the supreme advance of recent man (*Homo sapiens sapiens*), but rather the higher development of the creative abilities of the prefrontal cortex, is evidenced by the lack of art with **Neanderthal man.** Living in the North under conditions of repeated ice-ages, and stemming from *Homo erectus, Homo sapiens neandertalensis* had, on the average, as much as 200 grams more brain than recent man, but had a smaller prefrontal brain (Kornhuber 1993) and, thus, did not develop an advanced culture. After 200, 000 years his stone tools were almost the same as at the beginning, and although he had speech and could master the fire, he did not develop the art of cooking and, therefore, kept a mighty set of teeth and strong chewing muscles. It could not have been the climate, for he was better adapted to cold than recent man, who had come from Africa, and under the same climatic conditions in Central Europe around 40 000 BC developed many new tools as well as arts (cave paintings of expressive naturalness, sculptures) and a logging system for the phases of the moon. The Neanderthal man, however, who had more temporoparietal association cortex, retreated to the South of the Iberian Peninsula and became extinct. The present state that there is only one species left from the genus *Homo*, is the result of the dangerous creativeness of man. But instead of there being several species of *Homo* there is now a great variety of personalities.

In the **frontal brain** too, there exists a **functional differentiation of the cerebral hemispheres**, similar as in the temporal lobe: the left one is predominantly in charge of the verbal tasks, the right one dealing with the spatial-motor and the regulation of drives and emotions (Lee et al. 2002); this is also shown by the brain potentials with volitional effort (Fig. 4.2 and 4.3). However, the compensation (by the other side) of a loss of skills in the case of unilateral lesion is much better in the frontal lobe than it is in the temporal lobe in an adult with speech disturbances; this is perhaps because speech is learned early in life, whereas the will develops over many years, mostly as late as in puberty and, in part, even later.

A **biological basis of our freedom**, which we share with animals and which so far computers do not have, is the **spontaneous self-repair of defects in the brain**. In older age we all have little vascular infarctions in the brain which we are not aware of and which are compensated by repair programs. This works to the extent that blind people who lost their eye-sight early in life jointly use their visual cortex, in order to read the Braille script, which they feel for by touch (Uhl et al. 1993). Thanks to its cooperation with other brain areas, the visual cortex in such blind people is morphologically intact, whereas the optic nerves and tracts are atrophied (Breitenseher et al. 1998). Upon such processes of cooperation, circumvention, and reprogramming, rests the size-proportional effect of brain lesions on intelligence—first discovered in rats by Lashley but also valid (besides localisation-specific effects) in man (Kornhuber, Bechinger et al. 1985). Such a hyper-complex organ as the brain would not be operative without such self-optimization. **These self-healing processes of the brain** are, however, **dependant upon our own activity** (Held & Hein 1963), which elicits neurotrophic factors. In other words they **depend on our will**. As the proverb goes, a rolling stone gathers no moss (Of course this does not debase sleep and the useful transient shift of the vegetative nervous system after a meal towards trophotropic activity). Therefore the **creative enthusiasm** of grown-up people with meaningful action and the **pleasure of doing**, a positive feedback, and of **children when playing**, all that serves the self-development of their brains.

Chapter Eight

The Will and Dream Sleep, Feelings, Drives, Meaning-Happiness, Beauty, Love, Empathy and Theory of Mind

Similar considerations apply to the **dream sleep**, in which the brain is activated by random hits of impulses (stemming from a small assembly of nerve cells in the brain stem, which has nothing to do with drives) and thus—being cut off from the world—produces bizarre stories: Self-development and self-maintenance of nerve cells by exercising in the dream sleep phase is a more realistic theory than that proposed by Freud, Jouvet or Francis Crick (Kornhuber 1984b), especially considering that the life of infants consists predominantly of dreaming. The activity of nerve cells goes hand in hand with the secretion of nerve growth factors (e.g. the brain-derived neurotrophic factor), the glia cells at rest do not only provide energy-supplying molecules, they also, in effect, clean the brain. As far as creativeness is concerned, however, one must not expect too much from dreaming. Great discoveries are made during the conscious mental work phase. Kekulé's benzene ring was an exception. He did not have the idea during night sleep but during a short day dream only after intensely thinking about the problem.

Our **brain** is not a static system like a computer, but it is always ready to adapt to new challenges by **learning** and changing the biological fine structures. If it is not challenged enough, its abilities diminish. If one has adults wearing reversal glasses, they first have great difficulties walking and grasping, but after a few days everything is fine and some people can even ski with them (Kohler 1951). Control experiments with cats revealed that only active movements but not passive ones lead to re-learning (Held & Hein 1963).

The **feelings** and drives of man are by no means generated by the limbic system only. Presumably even the majority of feelings of man during creative activities are initiated in the frontal lobe, although the limbic system in the wider sense functions as an effector or a "soundboard." Children often play with pleasure and then one may have great difficulties to make them eat: the

joy hereby is the consequence of their own activity; it is positive feedback, in contrast to negative feedback, which underlies the saturation of drives (e.g. hunger), and which was erroneously regarded by Freudians as the epitome of all pleasure. Hölderlin e.g. requested in his poem "To the Fates": "Grant me just one summer, powerful ones, and just one autumn for ripe songs, that my heart, filled with that sweet music, may more willingly die within me. The soul, denied its divine heritage in life, won't find rest down in Hades either. But if what is holy to me, the poem that rests in my heart succeeds—then welcome, silent world of shadows! I'll be content, even though it's not my own lyre that leads me downwards. Once I'll have lived like the gods, and more isn't necessary." This feeling does not primarily come from the limbic system (which itself does not know art), but is initiated by the frontal brain. Goethe wrote in "Wilhelm Meister's Apprenticeship," "What is the highest happiness of mortals, if not to execute what we consider right and good; to be really masters of the means conducive to our aims?" This line is concerned with happiness as a consequence of doing right. Socrates, Plato and Aristotle had already seen this in that way and even with a view on human life on the whole: it is the honest life itself which is the happy life. According to John Duns Scotus too, happiness results from will. The fact that the feeling of happiness is mostly due to one's own willed actions, has been confirmed by empirical investigation by Czikszentmihalyi (1992). Karl Bühler (1929) called the joy of children playing, "functional pleasure" (*"Funktionslust"*). Nietzsche spoke of the happiness of the artists and philosophers and of *Homer's* happiness ("The Gay Science," vol. 4). It is, however, also happiness of the simple and honest man; one could call it the **meaning-happiness** of the creatives. It is not only functional pleasure, for it does not only restrict itself to doing good, but it also rests in our memory; a great deal of the **self-esteem** of internalized people is based on this. It is a piece of independence from the applause of others; it belongs to inner freedom, to a humane autonomy. Viktor E. Frankl correctly pointed out the great importance of the "will to meaningfulness."

Hesiod taught: "before virtue the gods have placed sweat," and Socrates saying: The honest, active life is in itself the happy one. After *work as punishment for sin* with the Hebrews, the Hellenistic experience was rediscovered in the Renaissance by the Humanists. Manetti, who, like Pico, saw creative achievements as a reason for human dignity, said (with reference to Aristotle's Nicomachean Ethics): "From the activity of man evolves much more joy than burden" (De dignitate IV 57).

However, not only happiness but also **the sense of duty,** taking care and many other feelings are initiated by the frontal brain; they can vanish after orbitofrontal lesions, whereas even a bilateral excision of the **amyg-**

dala (nowadays, erroneously hyped by Gerhard Roth as the center of the soul and having the last word on all decisions) causes symptoms only in the acute state, subsequently, however, compensation is rapid, so that the people affected are psychologically inconspicuous (see e.g. Anderson & Phelps 2002). Only by means of special tests can it then be ascertained that they perceive threat in facial expression or in utterances of fellow men less well than control subjects (Scott et al. 1997). If the amygdalae are excised in adult monkeys, they show less mistrust and are especially popular with their comrades (Emery et al. 2001). This is different, when the development of social behavior is changed through bilateral excision of the amygdalae in monkeys in early childhood (2 weeks of age): the young animals obviously experience disappointment by too much carelessness and then become more anxious in company with their fellow monkeys; but by no means do they become autistic, they are otherwise inconspicuous in their social behavior (Prather et al. 2001). Lesions that are restricted to the amygdala do not—in contrast to hippocampal lesions—cause memory disturbances (Zola-Morgan et al. 1989). We would not consciously experience feelings, which primarily come from the limbic system, without the cortex. The cingulate gyrus would at least be necessary.

Also, those feelings of happiness which arise from attentively looking at and listening to the **beauty** of nature and the arts do not primarily come from the limbic system but from the association cortex. They are also something specifically human, and thus were already seen by the great stoic philosopher of the will, Panaitius, as being components of humanity; from him comes the idea of "high humanity" (Pohlenz). By the way, also that other important feeling of happiness, whose lack in winter in the high North leads to suicide and depression, does not come primarily from the limbic system but from sunlight and its effect on the hypothalamus, the endocrine system and "the brain's chemistry."—All human feelings can be influenced by our own personal mind, and by cultural traditions and standards. It is to a lesser extent the intensity of certain feelings, which we also assume in animals (at least from the birds on upwards), it is their meaning and depth, which comes from emotional understanding, from higher values, from the insight into higher connections, and from discipline and faithfulness, which in man are provided by cortical functions. Naturally, it is not the prefrontal cortex alone that enables the limbic system to be humanized. Even for a function, which in monkeys the amygdala still fully control, such as the automatic warning about dangerous fellow members of the species, there are cortical fields available in man, in this case for the involuntary perception of dangerous voices in the auditory association cortex in the upper part of the temporal lobe (Grandjean et al. 2005), and for the warning about threatening faces in a temporobasal visual association field of the cortex, the fusiform gyrus besides the cingulate gyrus, the orbital prefrontal cortex and the amygdala (Vuilleumier et al. 2001).

The **amygdala**, a small assembly of neurons of about one and a half cubic cm in size (Brierley et al. 2002), is a phylogenetically old organ (the archistriatum of the reptiles), which is less well protected against epileptic discharges than the neocortex. It is a frequent site of origin of temporal lobe epilepsy with semiconscious psychomotor attacks, which are often connected with brief, involuntary actions and linked predominantly with anxiety. In epilepsy surgery it is successfully excised, mostly together with the similarly old and seizure-prone hippocampus; however, the latter must be excised only unilaterally since bilateral excision causes memory loss. But in man, after unilateral interventions, one does not see changes of impulse control, no addiction, no sensation-seeking and no decrease in anxiety. For anatomical connections of the limbic system, see Mega & Cummings 1994, and Heimer 2003. By the way, the amygdala is by no means in charge of all novelties; it specialized in the automatic detection of danger when dealing with fellow members of the species. For the general detection of novelties, which is of course essential to life, a much larger system is in charge of, it consists of the parietal cortex and the frontal lobe—including its limbic part (for the transfer of important information into long-term memory) which is the hippocampus (Knight & Nakada 1998). Besides the automatic surveillance of dangers that come from fellow species members, there are also neurons in the amygdala that influence autonomous functions and control evaluations of smells (Swanson & Petrovich 1998).

Having said that, we do not want to infer that the limbic system and the hypothalamus are unimportant; on the contrary, they are the **vital basis of the motivational system**, but its drives and the notification of needs (hunger, thirst etc.) are guided, in man, by reasoned will so that they can cooperate in a cultural-compatible way. Caring for the young, for example, is a biological drive, older than the human cortex of will, but even here, moulding of the instincts by the will can be seen: human helpfulness is not just a biological instinct. Sympathy, compassion, sharing somebody's happiness, in short, **empathy** in the humane sense is not possible without understanding someone else's emotions, without highly developed cortical functions, and with this partial function for establishing our will (nowadays called the ability for **theory of mind**) the prefrontal cortex—besides the anterior inferior temporal cortex, which is specialized for face recognition—is also involved (Goel et al. 1995, Farrow et al. 2001, Sabbagh et al. 2004, Iacoboni et al. 2005). Why is the understanding of the emotionality located frontally?—Because it belongs to strategy and the cooperation of people.

Not all drives are by no means phylogenetically old utterances of the limbic system; the critical **will for truth** of scientists and the creative drive of artists, for instance, are not conceivable without the great association cortex of man. Even the instinctive bond between mother and child, which is important for the formation of **confidence** and conscience, is—in man—not just a function of the limbic system, but develops along with the cooperation of the right orbitofrontal cortex (Schore 2000).

It is, however, not only the reasoned will that disciplines the drives, the process works the other way too; the will listens to the feelings, e.g. such a strong one as **love**, which is important for the stability of our course in life. A person, who does not know which people, homeland, traditions, and goals he loves, easily becomes drift-wood in the waters of the world. Love is the anchor; whoever lacks it is in danger of becoming histrionic. In the time before the advent of antidepressants, it was terrible to hear depressive patients lament that they could not love anymore. But also adoring love is not an automatic feedback regulation such as thirst, but develops with the help of judgment of values in the frontal cortex. It is humanized, personalized, and deepened by mind. It is senseless to play "heart" off against "reason": man needs both. Lack of sympathy can frequently be found; Europe was plagued for a long time, by lack of reason, today it is Africa. But surely these inner dramas unfold in the form of combats between passion and reasoned will.

Chapter Nine

The Will and the Limbic System, the Hypothalamus, the Arousal System, Circadian Rhythm, the Endocrine System, Fatigue and Impetus

The limbic system and the hypothalamus, the aminergic and cholinergic nuclei, the reticular activating system and the general impetus are important for the will. In the case of bilateral small vascular infarctions in the genu of the internal capsule, through which **afferent fibers** travel from the thalamus to the frontal brain, aboulia can result with apathy and stupor (Tatemichi et al. 1995, Namekawa et al. 1999). Even with unilateral insults in the intralaminar thalamic nuclei which transmit the **impetus of the reticular system** from the brain stem to the cortex, there are disturbances of attention and light disorders of the will (van der Werf et al. 1999). In such cases there is—because of the decreased neuronal activity—a decreased cerebral blood flow in the frontal lobe, a remote effect of the deafferentation. For the behavior as a mother, the medial preoptic area of the hypothalamus is important (Numan 1994).

The circadian rhythm, which affects wakefulness, mood, speed of thinking, willpower, the autonomous, endocrine, immune systems and body temperature, etc. surely has an influence upon the will. The circadian rhythm decides whether we are early birds or grumpy in the mornings, and how late we can hold out in the evenings without effort. The pace maker is located—in mammals—in the suprachiasmatic nucleus of the hypothalamus. Its neurons are synchronized with the earth's rotation by the light, if it exceeds certain intensity; melatonin plays a role. Sufficient sleep is important for both the body's health (e.g. immune defense) and the soul, including the will, and for good sleep darkness is necessary. Transcontinental flights across the degrees of longitude detune our inner clock. Continuous bright light has been used as a method of torture.

The **endocrine system,** which the limbic system also influences is important, not only for sexual behavior; an example are the **estrogens**; they have an antidepressant effect revealing itself by the fact that some women get depression after they have given birth to a child (the placenta is also a hormonal gland). Estrogens also act anti-psychotically (women have a later age of onset of schizophrenia than men) and offer some protection against dementia (Alzheimer's disease in women without estrogen substitution after menopause, is twice as common as in men). The effects of steroid hormones are derived in part from the vasopressin system in the limbic system (deVries & Müller 1998), which among others influences social behavior and the ability for friendship. On the formation of confidence, oxytocin has also an influence (Kosfeld et al. 2005). Hyperfunction and hypofunction of the thyroid gland, the adrenal glands and the pituitary, can cause severe psychiatric disorders, including disturbances of impetus. Hypothyreosis causes lethargy, hyperthyreosis causes overexcitability. Disturbances of impetus can also be caused by infections (to which also many chronic fatigue syndromes are belonging), by disorders of metabolism, latent depression and the effect of drugs and medication e.g. by dependency on benzodiazepines (Binder et al. 1984, Kornhuber 1988a). Organic disturbances of impetus are more frequent than inhibitions caused by neurotic conflicts of drives.

The most common avoidable **fatigue,** however, predominantly found in the elderly, is caused by the ingestion of large amounts of fast resorbing carbohydrates (e.g. potatoes). These cause a high increase of insulin secretion, and the insulin facilitates passing of the essential amino acid L-Tryptophane (competing with other amino acids) through the blood brain barrier. From tryptophane the brain produces serotonin, and this has a calming, sleep-inducing effect. The phylogenetic meaning of this regulation presumably is that the brain, which normally uses only glucose as energy source after a big meal, which ensures its energy supply for a while, can make the vegetative system switch from an ergotropic to a trophotropic mode.

The will is surely not almighty, but through **wise leadership** and through the **use of helpful activities** such as sleep, ambulatory activity, talking, taking medicine etc. it can help us to overcome hardships, and vice versa, the hedonistic "self-corruption" of the will is often the cause of decay and lingering illness. The **relation of reason, feelings and impetus** is complex, as is generally known, however, today, because of Freudian influences, the antagonism is overemphasized. Mostly they tend to harmony, whereby the will accepts suggestions of the feelings, and the drives fit themselves into the priorities set by the reasoned will. Man is despite some difficulties in dealing with himself, not a neurotic brain cripple, but, in fact, is so successful that he is today (in the western industrial civilizations) inclined to arrogance.

Chapter Ten

The Will Is Not Strictly Coupled with Consciousness

There Are Conscious and Unconscious Agendas in the Brain and Both Are Important

It does not help to play the **unconscious off against the conscious**. In the brain at any time most of the agendas are unconscious, much of it is, however, consciousness-prone. The conscious and the unconscious always work together, not only in dreams but also in wakefulness. Our conscience for instance can admonish us out of the unconscious core from our memory, but by doing so it becomes conscious, and it is then the task of the reasoned will to draw the consequences out of it. In the system of drives, there are positive drives (such as care for children) and those that are counterproductive (such as envy and greed); the will must come along with them all and thereby makes the person community-fit and culture-fit.

Surely there is **inferior behavior too**, when people let themselves be overwhelmed by instincts, such as vindictiveness, envy, vanity, greed and, above all, when the reasoned will is weakened (e.g. because of alcohol) or switched off by ganging up. In our decadent society hypocrisy is rampant, disguised as the intelligent will in service by hedonism. Here we see the back side of human nature which can also be a strong point of man: he is a family-being; incomplete brain development at birth and a long childhood make this necessary, and the evolution of cooperation as social hunters has made the **group influence** even stronger. The group dynamics go deep down into perception, thinking, belief and opinion; S. Asch (1951) and Elisabeth Noelle (1980) have investigated this influence. It is a sign of willpower to be independent in thinking, while keeping to the truth.

The adaptation of one's convictions to the group, **conformism**, also has genetic roots, however in first line it is a learning process. The weaker the self, the more conformistic one is (Hinkle & Wolff 1957) and the more rigid one clings to indoctrination effects. This holds not only for totalitarian states, this is daily reality also in democracies with their electronic mass media.—

For the effect of group pressure and indoctrination on the will, the self, cf. Kornhuber 1961.

The disharmonic cooperation of the limbic system and the prefrontal cortex in some people due to unfavorable genes can lead to **self-corruption** (Janzarik 1993), so that the intelligent will degrades to an accomplice of criminal intentions. In **forensic psychiatry** this is nowadays no longer judged solely according to the influences of psychotic disturbances but with a more differentiated approach, considering someone's life-story, situation, and how the subject acted before and after the criminal act: Preparing, planning, self-controlled waiting, purposeful elimination of traces etc. Not only the presence or absence of clear psychotic disturbances as the basis for criminal responsibility are investigated, but also positive signs of self-guidance are taken into consideration (Janzarik 2000); and of course, seduced children and immature youngsters are judged more mildly than purposefully acting adult criminals.

As far as **criminal law** is concerned we think retaliation as compensation for damages makes sense, and we adhere to **responsibility** and guilt in confirmed cases (i.e. in most cases). Punishment as a means of prevention, of education, and of the maintenance of the legal system is inevitable, although in detail the execution of sentences in its present form may seem to make little sense at times, and the detection rate is more important for prevention. But in law we do not only deal with single persons; man is a community being, he becomes human by cooperation. In the legal system we deal with confidence; this is the quality that makes society and humanity possible. One also has to consider that rights are always linked to duties. It is not just by chance that in the period of "Enlightenment" the philosophy of will reached a culmination point: at that time human rights were declared. The elimination of free will along with responsibility would throw us back to the dark days before the "Enlightenment." Perhaps law should see more than at present not only the momentary guilt, which is inherent in the deed, but also the lack of a person's own goodwill that has contributed to the development of the character of the culprit. On this difficult terrain there will always be errors, and not only because of ignorance and lack of truth, but also because of too much severity too much leniency, opportunism, pressure from the media etc. Children of schizophrenic mothers for instance, who are not manifest psychotic, are put in jail much more often than comparable persons from the average population (Heston 1966).

The way to improve such problems is, however, not to certify everybody insane but to do more for **prevention**, e.g. by education, job creation, etc., also by the help of medication in certain personality disorders, by earlier detection and treatment of psychoses and by a "health charge" on **alcohol**. During the Prohibition period in the United States, the excess mortality of men, which was basically due to alcohol-related violence, accidents, cancer and cirrhosis of the liver, disappeared (Kornhuber 2001), and during the Gorbatschow-Prohibition in the Soviet Union not only criminal activity went down but also the mortality of the Russians was reduced by half within three years and the excess mortality of males decreased (Leon et al. 1997, Shkolnikow et al. 2001); it is not necessary to put excessive pressure on a ban, because higher taxation of the destructive consumption is efficient. Prevention starts prior to birth, for alcohol and cigarette smoking have an effect on the brain of the unborn during pregnancy: today many children are born with the **attention deficit hyperactivity syndrome** (ADHS), a disorder of will, due to alcohol and cigarette effects during pregnancy (Kotimaa et al. 2003, Rowland et al. 2002, Mick et al. 2002, O'Malley & Nanson 2002). Today we have half a percent of children who have the full fetal alcohol syndrome (with the corresponding decrease in intelligence), which before 1968 was so rare that it was not even known to science, and approximately 5% of children are born with attention deficit, and we now have about fifteen times more alcoholism in women than before 1968 (Kornhuber & Füchtner)—representing a dramatic loss of freedom. Since 1968 girls smoke more (Kornhuber 1982) now as much as boys. Alcoholism of mothers and children has increased to the extent that there are already young people who have "age-related" diabetes (i.e. type II). We now have, in Germany, more than 100,000 alcohol-dependent youngsters and annually 25,000 youngsters are hospitalized because of acute alcohol intoxication. The more profound reason was the decrease in responsibility for children due to "the pill" (introduced in 1965), the trigger was the Vietnam war, the ideology was the hedonistic Freudo-Marxism of 1968. ADHS is not only a severe disorder in children but also it jeopardizes will in adulthood; it shows up in tests as a frontal brain disorder (Lovejoy et al. 1999) and often leads to alcoholism, drug dependency and crime (Molina et al. 2002, Tapert et al. 2002). Alcoholism and diabetes lead to early dementia.

How does will develop in the child? Will needs more time than the sensory systems, because the frontal cortex needs longest to develop dendrites and synapses. It is true that the neurons of the frontal cortex are already there in the infant, but their activity (as measured with the glucose consumption) is still very low. Between the 6th and 9th month of age the so-called *delayed response* starts to function, a sign that the working memory in the prefrontal cortex is becoming active; from then on, the glucose consumption increases (Goldman-Rakic 1987). Will does not awake until about the third year of life, prior to this, the parents have already worked educationally by admonition, praise and reprimand, love and reassurance. "The parents have the duty and the right to take care of the physical, mental and in particular also the moral education of their child" *(Motive zum Bürgerlichen Gesetzbuch,* Motives for the civil code, 1888, cf. Brezinka 1987)—and the children have the right—which has to be added in Pestalozzi's sense—to receive an education of their mind and will; it has taken a long time before the rights of children were acknowledged.—The further development takes place under the cooperation of the willed self-activity of the child and adolescent, whereby the will encourages itself by doing something successfully. The formation of the connections in the frontal brain continues for quite some time into adulthood, and new synapses can still be formed even in old age. The very long childhood with high plasticity of the brain structures through learning, and the influence of culture, above all of the family, is a decisive strength of man. A chicken can run immediately after hatching, it can peck and it sees the grains; a child needs three years to use a spoon without spilling something, and even longer to develop its will. Similar as previously when the child was happy to learn toddling, running and throwing and exercised this with pleasure; it now exercises its will, partially so by saying "No!"—This is contrariness, and now the child is in its **difficult age**. Children who are weak-willed at 6–7 years have—in 80% of the cases—not experienced this phase of negation, according to Hildegard Hetzer 1987. This will may not be broken; it must be encouraged and steered with love, example and firmness towards reason and sincerity. The child has to discover that self-control, carefulness, a sense of responsibility and strength of decision are virtues which bear reward in themselves. Areté, virtus, virtue, moral fitness have been named, which means: the basic position for the will to be good. Not spoiling but instructing is necessary but combined with goodwill, with reassurance of the good, with continuity.

The differences in will are much greater than in walking or in intelligence; these differences in self-control, fairness and depth, also play a great role with tasks often considered purely cognitive (Lee et al. 1983). **Frontal brain tests in children** show that the functions of wilful attention, of self-control, etc. from the second year onward improve continuously (Espy et al. 1999). The fact that a child is ready for school at the age of five or six, is due to the **self-organization of will** by playing, doing, learning, trying and setting goals to oneself. In a visual searching test, in which the target has to be found under distracting stimuli (i.e. a concentration test) a 5-year-old child already reaches the score of an adult. In the Tower of Hanoi-Test (with only three instead of four disks) the adult performance is already reached at the age of six, in the Wisconsin Card Sorting-Test at the age of ten. However, in the Tower of Hanoi-Test with four disks, adult performance is not reached until adulthood (Welsh et al. 1991). Significant progress of the performances in frontal brain function tests is made not until puberty (Levin et al. 1991). The will needs, like the fibers, dendrites and synapses in the frontal brain, many years for full self-organization. The functions of the posterior lobes of the brain—perception and speech—mature by playful learning, encouraged by the parents, earlier than the will. This enables communication with the adults and their prudence, which helps the will in its development. Children try to support their will themselves by activating the posterior brain areas, among other things, by speaking to themselves. We find this phenomenon of giving a voice to the inner dialogue again in older people having incipient troubles with memory and planning; and **verbal self-encouragement** is also an element of psychotherapy. In infants, a damage to frontal lobe, when the will is still underdeveloped, can initially pass unnoticed, but then it makes itself increasingly felt as a will disorder (Eslinger et al. 1992, Anderson et al. 2000). Especially if the self-control of the behavior is disturbed—a key function, for which particularly the right frontal lobe is important—a lot of sequelae of a cognitive and of a social kind are caused (Jacobs & Anderson 2002).

The **further formation of the will** then occurs predominantly by learning from persons who are **examples**, whom the children and adolescents are following but also by voluntarily setting goals, by challenging themselves, by own effort, by self-exploration and self-finding by the experience of *happiness by feeling sense*, by *"meaning-happiness"* (i.e. the inner happiness about the meaning of one's life), and by experience and by communication. With "drill" or rote little can be achieved, for it prevents self-initiative: therefore the maieutic (mentally "obstetric") method was suggested by *Socrates* which aims at stimulation of deeper thought and the formation of will by the person itself, and the principle of freedom in Humboldt's educational system was recommended. Of course these include one's own experiments, learning from error and success, cooperation and Platonic enthusiasm, as well as Aristotelian practicing. Concert pianists and competitive sportsmen know how much exercise is necessary to achieve the kind of performance that appears effortless. But the spark of that particular earnest enthusiasm, which people with mental will possess, often spreads only in familiar talk, as *Plato* wrote in his seventh letter. Socratic education, as rediscovered by Kierkegaard, is summarized by Jaspers (1977). The imperative of self-education of the will is coined by Pindar in his famous verse: Become who you are. What matters is: to actively accept the challenges but not let oneself be corrupted. The shining example in the ancient world was Heracles, the ideal in the time of Goethe, Iphigenia.

Learning to think requires courage as does learning of what I will, what I want. **Children learn this courage** (some need to be persuaded) **by their own doing**, and they also learn for their self-leadership **to observe standards and values**, and thereby gain freedom through the ability to cooperate. Will is not only an inhibitor but also a discoverer, continuer and completer. Thus it saves us from chaos by bonds to rule and order which cannot be reached by force, as long as the convictions are controversial, but only by insight and goodwill, at least for the majority. "The moral virtue" Aristotle says (and this is also a term of the ancient world for reasoned will) "arises from getting used to it. We are granted virtues neither by nature nor by something contrary to nature, but we are disposed by nature to acquire them, bring them to completion, however, only by getting used to them ... We become just by acting justly, and brave by acting bravely" (Nicomachean ethics). What Democritus and Confucius had seen, pedagogy of the modern age since Pestalozzi and Fröbel has confirmed: Mere talking is of little help; only example and love are effective. An investigation among executives shows that such examples are not found among personalities of public life, but rather mostly in the private sphere; the qualities which convince are personal integrity and professionalism (Accenture-Study 2005).

In **therapy** we also talk about will making somebody see sense, e.g. with addiction, phobia and obsession (Süllwold 1977) or depression. Clarity of will, self-motivation, getting things straightened out with oneself are great topics of psychotherapy, and are concealed in the term "*Sinn*," (sense, meaningfulness) in Viktor E. Frankl's Logotherapy. "If one has cleared up the Why of one's life, one can easily put up with the How," says the philosopher of will, Nietzsche. Then it is true what Dostojevski wrote about his Siberian imprisonment: "Yes, man is tough. He is a creature which gets used to everything and this is, I believe, the most appropriate description of him." It is certain that psychic stress and strokes of fate cause severe cyclothymic depressions as well as neuroses (Kornhuber 1955, 1962), also certain is that herewith the kind of psychic processing, and willed orientation towards the future also play a role (Allport et al. 1941), although it is clear that we are dealing—in the case of major **depressions** and bipolar disorders—with organic brain diseases (Baumann & Bogerts 1999), and that a genetic susceptibility is implied. By now at least one mechanism is known, by which stress hormones lead to depression: the inhibition of neurotrophic effects and the regrowth of nerve cells in the hippocampus. This is probably the reason why antidepressants need about two weeks to take effect and change someone's mood (Malberg 2004). In the case of depression in old age, there is generally a slight cerebral atrophy (Schweitzer et al. 2001) obviously because of microangiopathy. If not actively treated, these depressions, which are accompanied by a reduction in activity, impose a risk of dementia. Paralysis of the will is a vicious circle: it can inhibit the whole brain via the remote pathways of the frontal lobes (Price et al. 2001). By simply encouraging the hope that the patient can make it, one is already helping addicted and depressive patients threatened by relapse; to make them getting used to daily activity out in the sunlight also has a positive effect. Nietzsche and *Griesinger* have already noted the **will-strengthening and antidepressant effect of self-activity.**

Controlled science has confirmed these impressions (Taylor et al.1985, King & co-workers 1989). Inactive people develop twice as many depressions as people who have regular exercise outdoors. Not to give up is the first rule, search for clarity the other; both address themselves to will. Strengthening one's will by **concentration** is an old wisdom of doctors, philosophers, monks, and samurais. The masters of Buddhism have elaborated for this their own teaching tradition: **Zen**, self-liberation by concentration but without solipsism, in relaxed harmony which, in Japan, became the basis of the mental elite, with wide-ranging effects, as far even as painting. Goethe believed will was capable of influencing the immune system: Regarding a situation bearing the risk of infection he said (to Eckermann on April 7, 1829): "It is unbelievable, what the moral will is capable of in such cases! It penetrates the body, so to speak, and brings it into an active state which repulses all harmful influences." Of course, will plays an essential role in sport, in management and in research as well. Sportsmen often speak of concentration but also **endurance** and the **bearing of pain** are important. For therapy confidence in being able to help and control oneself has to be practiced, e.g. not to hush up the fact for oneself that a relapse into depression is impending but to immediately resume therapy. Mental activity has an even stronger effect on the brain than physical activity: it works in a developing, preserving and antidepressant manner, also preventing dementia.

Even **weak-willed patients due to brain damage** can be helped by well-aimed practice (Levin et al. 2000). Chronic alcoholics often have a disturbance of will (Ihara et al. 2000), which complicates their permanent weaning. It was harmful for them that therapists had lost their belief in the will and tried to evade this task. For stabilization and long-term encouragement non-professionals must also be recruited; self-help groups are important. As far as children are concerned the cooperation of the parents is of course necessary for therapy, especially that of the mother. Such therapy by the mother (under the guidance of teachers) can be very effective with the frequent disorders of speech in children. This has been shown by a controlled study, with a large control group (Bechinger et al. 1984). The assumption that the orbitofrontal cortex plays an essential role in addiction has been supported by imaging methods (London et al. 2000). The encouragement of will, self-reasoning and self-confidence is a central issue of all education, especially with disabled children.

Strengthening someone's will by doing something is a basic principle of **rehabilitation,** practice after injury, e.g. after a stroke, but also secondary to injuries or inflammation of the spinal cord which lead to a *neurogenic bladder*, a very molesting disorder. The most frequent cause is multiple sclerosis. In earlier times the patients died from the ascending pyelonephritis, later a permanent urinary catheter was administered, which, however, led to a chronic inflammation of the bladder. One must strengthen the will to self-help and the patients and their relatives should be instructed how to self-catherize using sterile atraumatic disposable catheters, in addition they should be taught to practice their bladder and control residual urine using ultrasound, because the disorder is inclined to relapse because of residual urine and overstretching of the bladder (Kornhuber & Schütz 1990). Also with patients suffering from chronic psychiatric illnesses, strengthening of the will by self-activity is important; an early pioneer on this was Simon (1927/29) with his work therapy. Recently it was found that its positive effects can be improved by additional neurocognitive enhancing practicing (Bell et al. 2001). This also improves someone's working memory.

Not only with therapy but also with **prevention** which needs the patient's active cooperation by keeping to a **diet and staying active,** exercising one's will over and over is required. For instance with hypertension, overweight, diabetes, after myocardial infarction etc. will is important and, as already emphasized, will and its encouragement, is crucial in the case of **weaning of addictions** (including cigarette smoking). The weaker a person's will, the more the free self-determination of man is endangered, above all so in childhood and adolescence. This is which the **seducers** are aiming at: the **weakening of the will** and they are commercially organised: Alcohol, cigarettes, drugs; starting at the age of twelve (Kornhuber 1982); dealers at school gates and in discotheques. There are also some sects which strive for weakening their members' will by dependence. Addictions are today worse than psychoses, since neuroleptics and antidepressants have been available. Heroin also contributes to the transmission of the HI-virus. Part of the people in the new lower class, who have lost their will to do better, have dropped out because of drugs. Their will was broken not because of unemployment but by toxic brain damage. Their families suffer with them.

Substance no. 1 and enemy of freedom no. 1 in Europe is **alcohol,** whose danger potential is played down in an absolutely unjustified way (Kornhuber 2001). Among other things it is a contributory cause of arterial hypertension, diabetes, stroke, dementia, accidents, violence, criminal acts and brain damage already prior to birth. A similar damaging effect on the development of the brain has smoking during pregnancy. It is erroneously believed that alcohol is a remedy for relaxation; in reality it is one of the avoidable main causes for stress, since it increases heart rate and blood pressure; the wrong impression of alcohol causing relaxation comes from disinhibition. For **stress management,** it is better to hike, to swim, to paint, to sleep and to think thoroughly in quiet surroundings about one's problems. Tranquilizers such as the benzodiazepines, however, are also not harmless, they have an addiction potential (Binder et al.

1984, Kornhuber 1988a). The legal drugs, loved by the powerful advertising world of today, and which the political parties in Germany close their eyes to, are also a bad example which the adults set for the youth; they pave the way to cocaine and heroin. Another point not noticed enough yet is **unemployment caused by substance addiction**. From this a long lasting vicious circle develops—unemployment increases discouragement, and this complicates overcoming the addiction. Prior to the advent of effective medicines against depression, anxiety disorders and schizophrenic psychoses (until about 1955), these predominantly genetic diseases, were the most common disorders of will. The life time prevalence for depressions is about 12% or higher, for anxiety disorders it is on the whole—a heterogeneous field—similarly high. The suicide rate was considerable, also with schizophrenia, which was less common but often chronic. Now addictions are the bigger problem, particularly if one includes nicotine addiction and the low dose dependence on alcohol which actually causes more damage than the well acknowledged high dose dependence, because it is 20 times more frequent. Besides, it is especially the low dose dependence (played down as "psychological" dependence) which lasts for years, whereas the physical dependence, which, upon withdrawal, leads to tremor, stops within days. It has a different neurochemistry: aminergic transmitters and receptors do not play the main role, but it is a sensitization of glutamatergic information transmission in the mesolimbic system (Schmidt 2000), which is predominantly responsible for the context dependence of the craving. Acamprosat, a medicine that makes relapses less probable, acts on the glutamatergic system.

In the future, because of the increasing longevity of people, **dementias** will be the main problem; they are also partially due to the so-called "normal" alcohol consumption (Fratiglioni et al. 1993, Yoshitake et al. 1995), among other causes acting by elevating blood pressure and the homocystein level (Bleich et al. 2001) as well as through insulin resistance (Boden 1993) and diabetes (Kornhuber 2001). Without memory will becomes helpless. The prevalence of dementia at the age of 65 is about 3%, thereafter the prevalence doubles every 5 years. The average life expectancy in Europe increases annually by a quarter of the year. The vicious circle is started by amyloid deposits caused by microangiopathy, which—in contrast to stroke—goes unnoticed (Kornhuber 2004). All risk factors for Alzheimer's dementia beyond the 65th year of age are causes of microangiopathy.

Disorders affecting will constitute a large part of **neuro-psychiatric diseases**, and the neuro-psychiatric field has a much stronger **economical impact** than the public is normally aware of, particularly if the loss of working hours and the nursing fees are counted as well. The expenses are, for Europe, now probably about 600 billion Euros per year (CDBE 2005). Alone with therapy this problem cannot be solved; we need much more effective **prevention**. For this the development of the will plays the crucial role.

Disabled people e.g. due to brain damage in early childhood often have all sorts of chances to develop and make valuable contributions, if one helps them (Hellbrügge 1981) and if they grasp the positive possibilities they have, using their own will to create something good with their own abilities. One may read e.g. the moving lecture of the psychiatrist Peter Willers Jessen at the meeting of the Society of German Natural Scientists and Physicians in 1846 in Kiel. At that time, the psychiatric sick lived in asylums isolated from the healthy people, and the psychiatrists lived with them. "I freely confess that I respect emotionally disturbed people more than others," he said.

There is, on all levels of society, a **humane nobility, which develops from long-lasting goodwill** (Kornhuber 1992). Confucius taught this, nobility was a main term with him: not nobility by birth but for the person, who has educated himself to be good. With the Stoics it was the wise man. Empirical social science speaks of strong personalities, who are opinion leaders in their circle as well, independent of their social class (Noelle 1997). Youth psychology has revealed that the exemplary quality of leaders of youth groups rest in their natural authority, always on duty for their sake and in authenticity.

In the inner leadership by the will, in conjunction with the creative abilities of the frontal brain, there lies freedom to find new solutions, **freedom** not against but with **nature**. An escape from nature is not possible; also for mental activity, which is information processing by changing the order system, energy is necessary. Will does not stand above the brain, the mind is not positioned behind the brain. For example, in the case of an injury to the retina of the eye the visual brain (the visual cortex in the occipital lobe) sees the defect as a dark scotoma. In contrast, an acute loss of function of the whole visual cortex (by bilateral infarction of the calcarine artery) is not perceived: the patient is blind, without experiencing that he is blind (cortical blindness, also called "blindness of the soul"); he even denies his blindness and invents something should he be asked about the weather. Only days or weeks later does he learn that something is not in order with his eyesight, but he is unable to perceive this, in contrast to a hole in the retina. In the same way **our emotional sphere** does not live outside the brain, it is rather the **inner aspect of the information processing in the human brain**; conscious vision in man is a function of the cerebral cortex (in frogs it is still a function of the optic tectum of the midbrain, but frogs do not possess a consciousness that is similar to man). With our conscience it is similar, if this disappears secondary to a lesion of the frontal brain, the patient does not take notice that it has vanished; he can happily tumble into joke cracking (*"Witzelsucht"*) and other symptoms—by painful experience and practicing he can, however, gain insight.

A disorder of conscious experience of cognitive defects from brain lesions, called **anosognosia**, lasts longer with lesions of the parietal lobe (Stuss & Benson 1986), longest, however, after lesions to the prefrontal cortex, and what is more, in the orbital cortex as well as in the dorsolateral one (Benson & Stuss 1990). This has also been confirmed for Alzheimer dementia (Reed et al. 1993). Surely there is also a psychological tendency to obscure problems to oneself, but an organic dysfunction of will makes it difficult for the **will for truth** to come to **insight** and to take up the challenge, which is important for therapy and prevention (Flashman 2002).

A concept that considers the **mind** an independent being, independent from the brain, has been haunting the theories since Plato, and one believed him, the great and pure one, particularly since he linked it with immortality. Even Leibniz ("Monadology"), who was well versed in computers, thought the mind could not just be created by the cooperation of the parts of the brain. Plato's theory even today—though in the meantime it has become much more abstract—calls the resistance of the realists, who then at times tend to throw—together with such "substance-mind"—also freedom overboard. Great influence he gained in modern age—not without some absurdity—by a scientifically thinking great brain, who thought that in the case of doubt he could trust solely on the consciousness of his own thinking: through the dualistic philosophy of Descartes (1641). The **body**, this concept says, is **spatial**; however, the mind is not. The **time-relatedness** of the mind is not entirely denied, for it must take effect on the body, but its relation to time is completely abstract, obviously it is even faster than light. On the real human mind, however, this does not apply. Neither our perceptions nor our imaginations can be absolutely spatial, although **our mind** has a **tendency towards unification**—obviously because this was phylogenetically favorable for survival, since disagreement inhibits action. Even if a person (after an operation, which cuts the connecting fibers of the two cerebral hemispheres within the corpus callosum, so-called split brain) in special experimental situations can reportedly have two independent streams of consciousness (Sperry 1974), he does not notice this splitting but feels himself a unity. Nevertheless, without spatiality the mind cannot get by in a spatial world. Not only our perceptions, also our imaginations have top and bottom, front and rear. In fact, we notice that our thinking takes time, but how the relation is between consciousness and time, remains a secret to us to a large extent.

The Platonic-Christian idea is that the activity of the mind precedes that of the brain, but since the mind is envisaged as immaterial—meaning that it is thought to be without energy—this is not possible, for mind is order, and putting something into order requires energy. It could perhaps—theoretically—at the most be simultaneous, in reality however, our **consciousness follows** slightly behind most brain activities, because it requires a great expenditure in cooperative activity of neurons. An excitation of the neurons of our retina (which is a part of our brain extended forward) takes, depending on dark- or light-adaptation, about 60 milliseconds or more to excite our visual cortex, and for the further processing towards a conscious perception, it takes even more time. With auditory and tactile perception, the conduction from the receptors to the cortex is slightly faster, but the processing in the brain requires approximately the same time and even longer with complex problems. The simple motor reaction time to a visual stimulus lasts in adults about two tenths of a second, in children longer. For a technical computer this would be very slow, but the strength of our brain does not lie in speed but in simultaneous processing in many partial systems with the utilization of great background knowledge.

Let us just consider speaking: While one syllable is uttered—for which a highly precise motor organization with specific programs as well as auditory and tactile regulation via feed back is necessary, without which the sharp transitions of the frequencies at the beginning and at the end of the phonemes would be incomprehensible—one has to prepare not only the next syllable of the word but also the whole sentence. Consciousness has to supervise this enormous expenditure of information processing and, if necessary, has to intervene with corrections. Because of "parallel processing" i.e. carrying out many steps of information processing simultaneously, statements about "before" and "after" and "simultaneous" of events in the brain are difficult (Conrad & Kornhuber 1967), particularly since there are delays because of conduction and multiple chemical reactions.

Consciousness under these circumstances is not at all powerless but essentially important, because it enables activity which is inspired by knowledge and problem solving with an overall view. A brain-injured patient, who does not regain consciousness, cannot just by living for a long time in this state compensate for his deficiencies, but he can, if he regains consciousness. The brain is an immensely complex composition, in which many things are tried out spontaneously. What is going to be durable depends upon what passes, in the light of consciousness, the **test at the outside world**. Without this permanent corroboration, the brain would be ungovernable. The realisation that consciousness is so important, is not only due to the fact that it facilitates learning, selection and freedom but also due to the fact that it does not do everything alone but it delegates most agendas to unconscious subroutines that have been available in the realm of living beings long before man's existence and which lead, if necessary, again to cooperation with consciousness. Burdening consciousness with the entire information processing would mean to overcharge it completely. The fact that it is, among the causes in the brain, not under the first ones temporally, does not lessen its efficiency—on the contrary, it means that it remains undisturbed by many random swayings of neuronal activity and is protected against quite a few false alarms by many pre-placed thresholds and filters, so that it can devote itself to the really important projects. The creativeness of man, however, to which consciousness contributes so much, has made man a danger to the life on earth; he has already caused the extinction of many species of living beings. Thus, the devaluation of consciousness (for instance declaring it an "epiphenomenon") is not an appropriate way of dealing with it. What is necessary is a humane education and making use of it in a wise manner (regarding consciousness as an "epiphenomenon," also see Delacour 1997, for discussion about the theory of consciousness Steinbuch 1965 and Dennett 2005).

Chapter Eleven

The Will

Is It Grounded upon Freedom or upon Total Determinism?

The notion that man is a mentally superior being is not only a fact, but above all the **obligation**, not to cause—by abusing his intelligence—damage to life on earth. The basis of this superiority is, however, not his bipedal gait, it is also not the ability to experience pleasure or the limbic system (that in man has not essentially changed as compared to the apes), but rather the **enormous development of his association cortex**, i.e. of those cerebral cortical areas that are not devoted to primary functions of the senses or to motor issues (Fig. 11.1). About half of these areas in man are devoted to will, the other half to insight and speech. Man does not only have more nerve cells in his association cortex than any other animal, including the dolphins, he also has, thanks to cooperation and speech, culture and a long learning childhood incomparably more knowledge. Unfortunately he has often used this superiority in an irresponsible way.

Man can do what he wants, but not will what he wants, said Schopenhauer—wrongly, for man can by no means do everything that he wants, but in many respects he can **learn to will what he wants**, if necessary with tools and aids (such as medicines). *Max Planck*, who founded the quantum theory and yet remained a man of the old physics, was of the opinion, that man was unfree if seen from outside, but free from inside, and he abruptly let stand this contradiction. However, this discrepancy of perceptions is usually not the case (except for intoxicated persons or disinhibited patients due to brain injury), and life and the laws demand from us that we correctly judge the **degrees of freedom** with ourselves and with others, e.g. when driving. Recently Bieri expressed a similar opinion about this (2001), who knows Kornhuber personally and got acquainted with his work at reviewer meetings for the German Research Council, which they both attended.

From malfunctions of the brain, from inner blockades, from omission of learning or simply from our mere dependency on the brain we cannot conclude that there is a general lack of freedom or complete bondage of man. **Total determinism is contradictory to itself,** for if our thinking were only a stream of molecules (in principle similar to the orbiting of the planets or peristalsis of the intestine), there would be no difference between lie, error and truth. If a totally determined person claimed, there were no freedom, this would be no more meaningful than a blow of the wind. Although we err many times, it can hardly be doubted that we will gradually come closer to truth, due to effective medicaments, functioning technology and the methodologically disciplined advance of research, whose investigations in many fields and insights from many sources fit together without contradiction. We ourselves have influence on the search for truth, in general on the information processing in our brain, also on instincts and feelings, albeit restricted: An optical illusion (e.g. the Fraser spiral illusion, 1908) persists in perception, even if we realize it is an illusion. It is a consequence of the mode of operation of the brain, which in principle does not copy but constructs actively, as *Kant* had already realized. And to speak with Cézanne: it is "parallel to nature." Similarly to this example from perception (as is the normal case), there are segmental errors in the instincts with some people, e.g. pedophilia; it is so far not completely curable, but can be alleviated by medicaments, so that it can be kept under control and thus becomes bearable for the man affected. It is untenable to conclude a total lack of freedom of the will from all this. Systems develop novel features, even technical ones, e.g. for self-control. One can also simulate creativeness technically, e.g. by the combination of rules with a random generator. But as life cannot solely be reduced to chemistry, the human mind is not fully predictable from the brain activity, in spite of the richness of psychophysical correlations.

If our life were totally determined, it would not be a task but an automatic scene of events, it would be simpler, but at the same time much poorer. There would be no scruples or shame, no meaning-happiness about great successes nor the many aberrations: hedonism, self-deception, histrionics, cruelty etc. In human life it is the ethics that matter, also truth, kindness, bravery etc. In view of the Janus head of freedom deep thinkers (among others Sophocles) considered whether it would not be better for man, not to have been born. Since he has become, however, the dominating being on earth, he cannot evade his duty, to behave in a humane manner. Without will to the better, goodwill, man is now in danger of becoming an evil to the earth. The appropriate measures that have to be taken are **linking the moral will to the sense of reality** (Reiner 1964). Goodwill, which persists, makes sense; already Kant saw the situation of man from this aspect. Our hedonisticly depressed

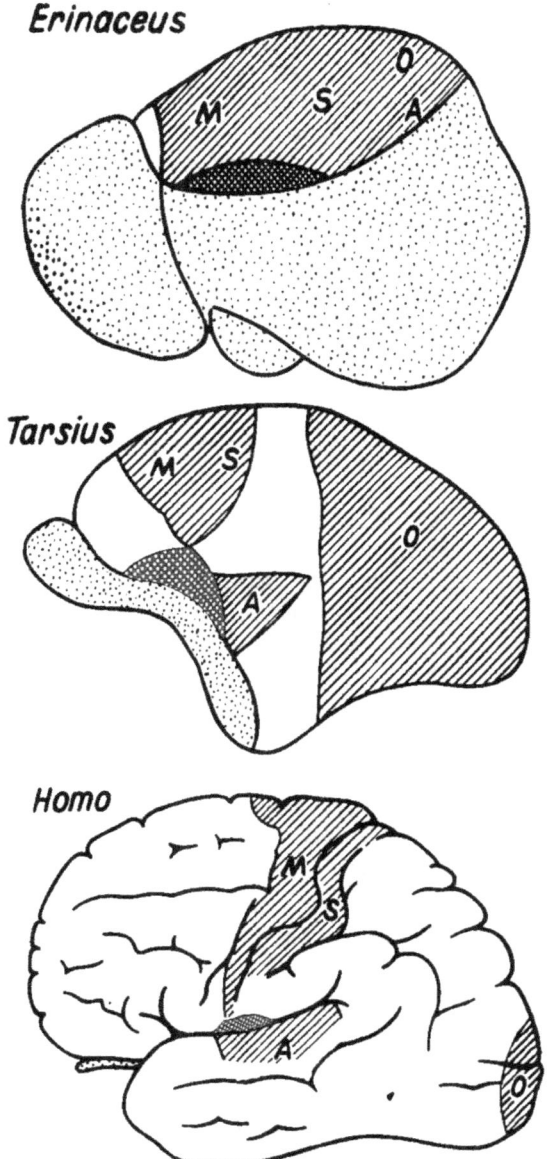

Figure 11.1. Evolution of Association Cortex. A comparison of the brains of the hedgehog, tarsier (a prosimian) and man shows the enormous development of the association areas (white). In the hedgehog, the olfactory brain (marked with dots) is large, with the tarsier the optic brain (O), in man, the association areas. Naturally his brain is on the whole larger; here the sizes are normalized, so that the relative partitions of the sensory (auditory A, optic/visual O, somatosensory S), motor and associative areas are emphasized [In part taken from: Starck D (1965) In: G Heberer (ed): Menschliche Abstammungslehre, Stuttgart, Gustav Fischer].

time needs ethical impulses which link the honest action to the sense of life, in order to set foot again on solid ground.

We do not only have to develop our will ethically, but also **preserve its vital basis**. To Plato's and Aristotle's cardinal virtues belonged—besides justice, prudence and bravery—also wisdom. Naturally our mind depends on the brain just like our life depends on many things: the sun, water, plants etc.—a completely independent freedom does not exist. We should not have smart disputes about determinism, instead we should strive to become better and develop and preserve our freedom, for many things threaten it: untruth, addiction, depression, brain trauma, stroke etc.

Some total determinists today insinuate that those contemporaries who stick for good reasons to responsibility have low motives. "There is no freedom of will," the Freudian Alexander Mitscherlich said, "this is an infantile invention of self-idealization." During religious periods with little knowledge and a risk of death the belief in providence (as till today in Islam) has the function of a sedative: "in God's hands"—today total determinism rather weakens goodwill and can become an accomplice of hedonism.

Those "exactly identical conditions" under which a free will, in the opinion of some logicians, must produce totally different things in order to be acknowledged as free, are unreal, never controllable, unnatural fiction, and the freedom, that is postulated there, would be an **unnatural miracle**, the associated will, however, would be an unreliable fellow, not a reasoned leader but a muddler all over the place, i.e. a *diabolos*. **Real freedom** (and also an experienced lack of freedom) is **natural and relative** (Kornhuber, 1984), for this, however, it has good reasons and it is efficient, e.g. curative or creating something beautiful. **Not arbitrariness without reason** but rather **choice of the authentic and good** characterizes freedom, and the **will** searches for and holds onto this, it **binds itself**. In neurophysiology, with which it deals and on which it depends, will works from "top" to "bottom" but not as a tyrant, rather as a good father, who also learns from his children, and keeps himself on the right path by prudence. It is interaction in a complex system, which is physical but also has consciousness and openness for the future.

It is an error common among philosophers today that the natural sciences are only responsible for the outer aspect, not the **inner aspect**, that of perception, feeling, thinking and acting of man. We need these terms from inner experience in order to interpret our brain physiological measurements. On the other hand, at times we need physical methods, measuring things from outside, in order to help each other or at least understand each other. One can e.g. talk to somebody for quite some time about a Picasso painting from his pink period and gain the impression that the person talking with experiences something different, until one discovers by an objective test that he has some kind of color blindness (which he might not have been aware of). The opinion that we all have a similar consciousness is only partially correct. There are people who have something like a hole in the place where in others sympathy is located; this cannot easily be recognized but in the long run their behavior reveals it. Especially the combination of objective neurophysiology and subjective psychophysics delivers elucidating contributions to the understanding of the human mind, on both the perceptive side (e.g. Kornhuber 1972) and on the side of will, which we have given examples for in this book. Some philosophers, however, have understood that one has to know something about the real world, of its reception by the senses and its processing by the brain, in order to understand the mind better; they now speak of "neurophilosophy"; their discussions about how *"Gedankenexperimente"* (experiments in our mind's eye) and other things work, can be found presented in an entertaining way with Dennett 2005. Quantum physics has shown that in the microphysical sphere, determination as *Newton* conceived it does not exist. There is, as Heisenberg found, pure chance and unpredictability, and research has shown that chance can have effects even when one goes up into macrophysics e.g. with the weather. The first natural scientists already acknowledged chance among the laws of nature. "Time is a child that plays," wrote Heraclitus, and Democritus went on to explain how, by random processes, order can develop, e.g. the assortment of pebbles on the beach.

However, **chance does not explain freedom**, for random behavior is not what we expect from a reasonable person. But it is true that the world of chance expands the scope of **fantasy** which man utilizes for innovations. For instance, what dreams tell us, evolves partially from the random encounters of the ascending activating impulses from the brainstem (from a small region without psychological or emotional content) to the cortex. The way how we spin these chance events to dream stories, however, is subject to our own personality and momentary emotional setting, upon whose composition we have not been without influence. Thus, the freedom of man is not an arbitrary example of indeterminism of physics but a consequence of our particular **brain organization** and **cooperation** and our own **efforts to develop these constructively**.

Similar as in the life of individuals, will is a great mover in **politics too**, as the liberation from dictatorship in the Ukraine has recently shown again: by self-discipline bloodshed was avoided. A shining example was the German unification, a historical achievement of the will for peace. In some states of Africa now every third person is infected with the HI-virus—a disaster for the children etc. In other African states, however, it looks much better due to the will of the governments for prevention. With the common formation of will it's not just about democracy which stimulates the will because of the possibility of cooperation but can also lead from one kleptocracy to the next, but it's also about the leadership of the law (Plato), about the separation of powers (Montesquieu), about checks and balances (The Federalist), about transparency as a means against corruption, about freedom and about humanity. The **subsidiarity principle** is founded upon the respect towards the reasoned will. Those solutions which can be contributed by oneself and decided upon in small circles, should be striven for in places, where one knows the people and can judge their reliability. It was not only Oswald von Nell-Breuning, one of the fathers of the Catholic social doctrine, but before him Baron von Stein, John Stuart Mill and Toqueville were thinking that way.

Rarely a single will has such eminent impact in politics as of Alexander's; usually a single will works via technical devices (e.g. Gutenberg) or in science (e.g. Darwin). Of importance is the tradition of the formation of will, e.g. the low corruption rate in Scandinavia. But traditions can also be changed as one presently sees in Eastern Europe. Non-governmental organizations are becoming more and more globally important because of their efficiency and lack of interest in power or profit. They show what voluntary engagement can produce in spite of increasing concentrations of power. There are, however, even in the jungle of the media, commerce, politics, and in the situation of the **organized lie** (Solschenizyn 1974, Revel 1990) which by no means has totally disappeared, again and again moments when courage and discipline of a single person can have unexpected success. Also necessary is obliging cooperation, following the example of the OSCE. By insisting continuously it has moved the Soviet Union to make concessions to human rights, which at the time of the decline of the power of the Bolshevists contributed a lot to managing the transition in a non-violent way. Similar influence could now have the Global Marshall Plan Initiative (2005): it postulates among other ideas a Tobin tax on international financial transactions (annually more than five hundred trillion US dollars, largely an economically senseless expression of speculative greed) to finance development aid, school education for all children, "mini credits" for women in poor countries and financial aid under the condition that benefiting countries fight against corruption, improvement of the law and of education. Community spirit and self-discipline of leadership elites in eco-social market economies are achievements of our will.

Although by the discovery of the Bereitschaftspotential in 1965 an impulse for investigations into will and into freedom was elicited—the terms volition, self-control and intention, which had disappeared by 1965 have continuously increased in the Psychological Abstracts since 1968 and reached about 70 investigations per year, by the end of the nineties; in addition, there are quite a few neurological publications about "executive functions"—and yet there is today a **new edition of the old propaganda for total determinism** (that passes off as original and, thus, impresses journalists) going back to two neurobiologists. One of them, Gerhard Roth, who worked predominantly on salamanders, is trying to persuade us to give up responsibility—with the untenable argument, the development of the human personality would be already finished at the age of three and would not change thereafter, thus suggesting that personality is only a product of the genes and of early childhood pre-conscious imprinting. Freudians claim that someone's personality has been fixed forever in **early childhood**. The check-up on this assertion by empirical investigations of Cecil Ernst and Nikolaus von Luckner (1985) did not confirm this. With regard to the person's commitment, not someone's early childhood but rather the life situation during someone's whole childhood is decisive. A backlog in development is not due to separation from the mother but comes when stimulation is below average. The development of behavioral disorders or delinquency does not depend on the early separation from the mother but on long lasting difficulties and burdens during the whole childhood and adolescence, whereby also a genetic vulnerability plays a role. Another well-controlled investigation of 47 persons who were taken to foster homes right after birth and spent their early childhood there, and of 50 control persons showed the following: They were all examined as adults (in their mid thirties) and a large pool of data—reports and testimonials from school, military service, occupation etc.—had been accumulated. They were re-evaluated "blindly" (i.e. without knowledge of their fates as children). The study revealed that although there were difficulties in some of the former foster children in childhood and adolescence, now as adults no differences were found between the two groups. The problems remaining in both groups had unambiguously genetic causes (Heston et al. 1966). The imprinting by someone's early childhood is overestimated. With admission into an appropriate family it is obviously possible in many respects **to relearn what has been missed in childhood**. As early as 1959 Hans Thomae summarized this in *Handbuch der Psychologie* (Handbook of Psychology) Vol. 3, 264: "Incorrect is above all that the human personality can be seen exclusively as the result of imprinting in early childhood." In psychological tests with twins, performances in a frontal lobe test such as the Wisconsin Card Sorting Test are inherited in only 40% (Anokhin et al. 2003). The skills required for performance in the WCST develop provably only in later childhood and, as with the personality factors, criminality etc., obviously self-education plays a role. Of course, this is not a *carte blanche* for bad treatment of children, but it corresponds to the fact of lifelong learning in man, albeit with a gradual decline in learning ability, if an appropriate challenge for this occurs (in elderly people e.g. a stroke or the death of the matrimonial partner), whereby it is well-established that for specific forms of learning e.g. for the acquisition of speech, there is a sensitive phase in childhood. For this reason hardness of hearing has to be corrected as early in life as possible. It is correct that one must utilize the great eagerness to learn of children in pre-school age, as is done in Japan, where the acquisition of four different scripts would otherwise not be possible. One should be on one's guard, however, to make a dressage out of it and neglect eliciting creativeness and the time expenditure for it. Already a reduction of television consumption would have a positive effect.

Another argument of Gerhard Roth for the total lack of freedom reads: the **Bereitschaftspotential** would prove the absence of **consciousness** with voluntary actions. The Bereitschaftspotential, being very small compared to the spontaneous brain waves, is the result of averaging over many stereotyped simple movements. The formation of will has already taken place prior to the start of the whole experiment, and the preparation for movement is initially handed over to unconscious routine processes of the basal ganglia, the supplementary motor area and anterior to it the pre-SMA (Deecke & Kornhuber 2003), which in turn do the groundwork for the motor cortex, which finally gives the command for the single finger movement. Even more remarkable is it, however, that consciousness is switched on about 200 milliseconds prior to the onset of movement, for each of the many simple stereotyped movements of the index finger. 200 milliseconds before movement onset are still in time to make changes, if necessary (Libet 1985). This is a great expenditure for the brain and shows that even such unimportant movements are controlled, if they are voluntary. Consciousness with its brightness and its freedom is known to be restricted and its time is valuable, only important events get access to it. Between the information flow in our senses and that in our consciousness there is a selection (and this sophisticated selection is also unconsciously organized) of the important matters—an enormous compression of information of at least 10^4, since through the receptors and afferent nerves at least 10^5 bit/sec (by order of magnitude) are flowing, in consciousness, however, only 10 bit/sec show up. The will, however, always takes part, albeit in that it delegates as much as possible to unconscious routines and expert systems.

Decisions in the brain are mostly not made abruptly—except we are forced by the situation, for instance when skiing—rather they are made gradually. Even simple decisions (for instance the pressing of a right or a left button) need some time, and a few seconds go by, until we start the movement. (The matter is different, if we are under time pressure or with rapt attention to a stimulus). This can be because we were not yet absolutely determined or because the way from the frontal cortex does not go directly to motor cortex, which was earlier belief, but needs the cooperation of a phylogenetically old subcortical part of the brain that provides learned and stored movement programs, the **basal ganglia.** Functional magnetic resonance imaging then shows vague activities, which can be interpreted as if up to 10 seconds prior to the movement in the prefrontal brain an unconscious decision had been made (Soon et al. 2008). This is not a sign for a lack of freedom, rather it signals insufficient attention or shortage of memory in conjunction with the absence of haste. The resulting movement is consciously controlled in any case.

Another neuroscientist, Wolf Singer, an expert of the visual system, who predominantly investigates cooperation of the nerve cells, is of the opinion that the principle of responsibility of man is untenable, for in the brain there is no leadership: "There is, in the brain, no location, where **decisions** are made." This is an odd argument for, already in the visual cortex, the information is conducted from level to level and even on parallel pathways simultaneously to different higher stations of processing in order to finally converge and travel to the frontal cortex, where the information, along with signals from other senses and the "system of the needs" flows into the formation of will and thus for the leadership of the whole human being. Naturally, the frontal brain needs the cooperation with other parts of the brain; but even if the sites vary in which precedence and subordinate decisions are made: Decisions exist in the brain. This is witnessed not only by our consciousness but also by our behavior. Singer is obviously using the argument that in the brain, as far as we know, no "grandmother cells" exist, thus there are no neurons that are specialized on the recognition of our grandmother, rather the neurons in varying groupings can serve different purposes. This argument, however, could be used just as well for the impossibility of perception as against will. The fact that there is perception has never been denied by Neuroscientists. Not even Berkeley has claimed total agnosticism. Science, in any case is not compatible with total agnosticism.

Surely we do not know everything yet, but some knowledge about the brain can be derived to a larger extent from psychology than from neurophysiology. We do not really understand the information processing in the cell columns of the cerebral cortex nor the coordination of their cooperation (Creutzfeld 1983, Mountcastle 1998)—and we have so far gained more insight from deficiency syndromes after lesions and from the electrical, magnetic and metabolic macro changes with the effort of will than from the changing activities in the network of the single neurons. However, what we know from pathology, physiology and neuropsychology does fit in with the anatomical connections. The information handled by the brain stems in part from the heritage of phylogeny, in part from sensors directed towards both the outer world and the interior (Kornhuber 1978b): this information is step by step processed into decisions, whereby metarepresentations of the world enable us to think independently from the world around us.

The largest body of experience about the abilities of man and his brain has been collected by clinical neurology. This experience has led to two theories (models) of how the brain functions: Firstly, **a hierachical system** of centers ordered side by side or on top of each other—in favor for this system are the specific functional deficits secondary to localized, acute cerebral lesions, also the results of functional magnetic resonance imaging and the capability of reasonable self-leadership of man. Secondly, since Lashley's (1981) "mass action principle," which does not hold for rats only but was confirmed also for man, namely for children (Kornhuber et al. 1985), **a distributed system**, in which, by nerve fibers, most of the brain is connected with many other centers, and this system achieves its performances always by distributed cooperation—in favor for this system are the associative memory and the gradual recovery of function (with the help of active training) after lesions but also the histology and hodology of cerebral networks.

Both principles are obviously realized in higher brains (Mountcastle 1998). In its activity the brain can achieve astounding performances, which we are mostly not consciously aware of: For instance the visual perception of a figure on a moving background requires numerous multiplications carried out in a decentralized manner in the distributed system of the brain. On the other hand, our ability to mentally go back the way in time of our own acting and experiencing and also the fates of companions in life, i.e. episodic memory, requires self-leadership with the high art of management, and this leadership is organized by the prefrontal cortex within the hierarchical system (Wheeler et al., 1997)—of course with the support of the distributed, associative system. The distributed system Singer is argumenting with, is nothing new, it is discussed by brain researchers and cyberneticists since long. But with its existence, which gives the brain great performance and high flexibility, a lack of freedom cannot be argued, on the contrary it is, similar as the hierarchical system, a rich source of freedom. We need both systems.—If one asks oneself which cortical field, on the basis of its anatomical and neurophysiological data, could be brought into consideration as a candidate for a leadership function, one could also think of the parietal lobe, for in parietal cortex many sensory messages (visual, somatosensory and auditory) from the outer world come together (Kornhuber 1965) and serve for the regulation of attention. But this cortical region lacks the connections with the old system of the internal needs and drives with its messages from the inner world, limbic system and hypothalamus. It is true that with lesions of the parietal cortex we get disorders of attention but no loss of strategic planning. Combining both, the messages from the outer world and from the inner world takes place in the frontal lobe only. Therefore, it is not a matter of chance that the further evolution towards a higher planning and decision center has taken place in the prefrontal cortex—with responsibility, with conscience. But instead of acknowledging these facts that are in agreement with the ethical wisdom of mankind since the Achsenzeit (Jasper's axis time), since Heraclitus and Kungtse, the spokespersons of the new irresponsibility try to argue away the autonomy of the mature man and are collecting, instead of arguments, allies for propaganda (Elf, 2004). Gerhard Roth even tries to discredit reason and sense and associates rationality not with ethos but simply with speech. He claims, it is the "level of self-description and self-deception, of diplomacy and lie, steered by, what is nowadays called, the guts (Roth 2008).

Furthermore, Singer thinks that the mere fact that the **human mind has a physical basis** proves that man is not free. This opinion is based on a term of freedom remote from nature: total freedom from nature. Real freedom is relative, contingent, specific, gradual and naturally acquired. This freedom is not an illusion, assessment by others and self-experience fit together, e.g. in the case of being tired. Only with toxic disinhibition or lesion-related lack of self-criticism are there illusions of freedom (to the extent—e.g. with LSD-intoxication—of the illusion of being able to fly, with lethal consequences at times). In the normal range, however, our conscious estimation of freedom is usually realistic—which is to be expected according to the selection process of phylogeny. Skeptics of will should think about the fact that freedom of will in the sense of conscious, intended self-control of human behavior (e.g. the so-called "social" alcohol consumption) has experimentally been confirmed beyond any reasonable doubt. (e.g. Howard & Myers 1989).

Wolf Singer draws extensive conclusions for our legal system from his dubious premises, he pleads for the abolition of **responsibility**. However, not all violations are drug-related crimes of heroin-dependents. Surely we need more prevention. But would anyone seriously claim that nobody were responsible for atrocities planned with the aid of high technology, counselled in many steps, and decided on a supreme level, such as atomic bombs released on cities (Coulmas 2005). Singer believes that with the abolition of responsibility the world would become more humane; the contrary is correct. This attitude would also abolish many high and honourable features of man: the human being would turn into a business conditioned by drill, dressage or diciplining. Profound thinking, self-sacrifice, devotion and bravery would then be illusions. Men honoured for millenia—men like Confucius, Socrates, and Jesus—would no longer be idols for enthusiastic following. And if everything became a matter of dressage, drill or disciplining, of a price and of propaganda, what would happen to the truth of science? Singer believes people would get accustomed to being not responsible. Very improbable, for they want to have autonomy and honor it. Without a moral will there is no moral behavior. Olivi saw correctly: without a will we would not be humans. Goodwill, by the way, also plays an important role for health, above all in prevention. An example for the maintenance of freedom is the examination of the newborn for intact thyroid function in order to prevent cretinism; without responsible physicians and nurses it can't be done.

Chapter Twelve

The Will

Its Freedom Is Not a Priori Granted: We Have to Do Something for It— Actively Increasing Our Degrees of Freedom

The fact that the system of will in the brain is a **distributed** but **cooperative** system, does not speak against freedom. Modern management is cooperation. The system of the senses, the motor system, the memory systems are also distributed and cooperative. This is a result of phylogeny. Mammals already lived during the times of the dinosaurs; new parts were added to their brains again and again. **Cooperation** for information processing is the basic principle in the brain; a single nerve cell is relatively stupid (although it can have a highly complex structure with connections to many other cells and it has an integrative function, it can possibly even multiply). One can easily make this clear with perception: the depiction of a punctual excitation on the retina of the eye upon the cortex could theoretically be carried out with little expenditure (*de facto* it is difficult because of dispersion and the changes in luminance), but already the perception of the length of a horizontal line requires the cooperation of nerve cells of both cerebral hemispheres with the help of the fibers of the corpus callosum connecting the two (Bechinger et al. 1972). Who ever denies the possibility of generating novelties by means of cooperation in the brain, negates not only freedom but already the possibility of simple perception.

It is not enough, as far as the freedom of will is concerned, to discuss only logical arguments; one must open one's eyes for the interconnection of freedom in nature: there are natural and cultural **causes** and **actions** that **support freedom** (e.g. a good education), and others that act against it; to name a simple and common cause: drunkenness. We have already experience with freedom, and we can and must do something for the sake of freedom. *A* great spirit of Goethe's time who saw freedom of man in a natural manner, like the ancients Hellenes, Hölderlin, said: "All man may examine ... that he is strongly nourished, thanks for everything, learns and understands the freedom to start off, where he wants."

It is also stupid to indoctrinate an aging society with the assertion, that it is not capable of learning. Daily physical exercise besides a careful early treatment of high blood pressure and of the tendency towards diabetes as well as healthy nutrition (green salads, a variety of fruit, vegetable oil, fish, vegetables, full grain, yoghurt, legumes, a little meat, nuts) and above all an appropriate mental activity at an advanced age are more than an efficient **prevention against dementia** (Kornhuber 2004). Dementia is, in our aging population, the greatest threat to our freedom. Our hedonistic lifestyle with alcohol, a lack of exercise and a paunch manoeuvers us into a position, from which dementia can take hold.

Contrary to an unsound blanket condemnation of the **estrogens,** we are pro substitution of hormones after menopause whenever deficiency symptoms should occur. Women without hormone therapy develop Alzheimer dementia more often than men, although it can be expected that men because of their behavior (alcohol, cigarette smoking), would have more vascular damage and, thus, more dementia, if this difference were not be balanced out by estrogen deficiency in women. Men—due to their destructive consumption—die seven years earlier (in Russia 10 years earlier) than women. Since many men do not outlive their dementia and women live longer, about 70% of patients with dementia are women. The results of epidemiological studies with estrogen-substitution are positive (Paganini-Hill & Henderson 1994, Morrison et al. 1996, Tang et al. 1996): Estrogen substitution therapy lowers the risk of dementia. Of course one should not prescribe estrogens to women who are at risk for breast cancer (incidence of breast cancer among first degree relatives). However, the unfavorable results of the Writing WHI group were not due to estrogens but to a harmful progestin, MPA, as well as due to the fact that therapy was begun ten years too late. The positive estrogen effect works via the vessels; the underlying basis of Alzheimer dementia beyond 65 (i.e. about 97% of all Alzheimer cases) is a microangiopathy (Kornhuber 2004). It is certain that estrogens act favorably at the arterial vascular system. Before menopause, women get heart attacks much less frequently than men. Only the combination of cigarette smoking and the pill is unfavorable, but the pill is not the physiological estrogen.

It is never too late to learn and to make one's lifestyle healthier. In order to fight against the widespread under-development of the right hemisphere, it is e.g. appropriate to do something practical, like holding the walking stick with the left hand, or painting and even singing. Instead of watching television for four hours per day, as is usual nowadays, self-selected meaningful activities do not only promote enjoyment of life but also **memory** at an advanced age.

Mental activity such as reading, solving puzzles, playing chess, playing a musical instrument, painting etc. offers even stronger protection against dementia than physical activity, and the effect arises independently from other influences (Wilson et al. 2002, Vergese et al. 2003), which is in favor of a direct action of the neuronal activity (probably with the help of neurotrophic factors). The basis for this has been laid in childhood and adolescence: In Chicago the dementia risk decreases by 17% with every year of further school education (Evans et al. 1997). **For all this man needs will** (albeit not will alone); he needs will also for **friendship, faithfulness** and mutual help which stabilize human life (e.g. Mäkinen 2000). The more a society ages, the more important practicing one's will becomes, for we need our will not only for the build-up of brain function and society, but also for their maintenance.

Damages to health caused **by our own behavior** constitute today a much larger part of total morbidity than in the 19th century; at which time, infectious diseases and accidents were the main problems. Diseases caused by self-destruction are still increasing, e.g. type II diabetes. Because of an aging population, the diseases caused by one's own inappropriate behavior have a much greater effect, the sequelae in the brain being particularly difficult to cure; they reduce our freedom excessively. Therefore, it is inevitable that much more **prevention** than so far is necessary. This, however, requires changes of behavior and **self-discipline**. The same demands hold for the solution of **global ecological problems**. Until now mankind has not even begun to free capital for their solution; part of it is renunciation. With the present hedonistic course, we are steering deeper into self-destruction.

Those who remind us of the possibility of goodwill are not illusionists of mere dynamics; we are realistic and see the tragedy too. But in a situation of failure, one must assemble, reconsider one's strategy and exert oneself over what is still possible.

Summary

Will is reasoned self-leadership of man, is thinking and acting out of one's personality and its core, the self, and responsible acting in the community. Will needs strategy, goals, reasons, methods. The will of man is creative and is supported by culture and cooperation. It is not an automatism of brain physiology but, imprinted by culture, it develops with the help of learning from examples, one's own initiative, and with the help of learning by trying and by reflection on oneself. Deeds of cooperative will are concealed in institutions of the law, of science, etc. Without goodwill, there is no fairness, no humanity. One risk for self-corruption, characteristic for man, is hedonism. Will is leadership, but it requires the basis of energy, alertness, etc. and many brain functions (memory and others). Will can and must do something to preserve these foundations. Not speech but noble will is the most precious commodity in man, and will is active in all realms of the soul. Thought, planning, decision, attention, caution, completion are part of will. Will generally cultivates a cooperative style of leadership in the realm of the incentives, drives and emotions, and yet important tasks of will are concentration on the most important issues and cutting out distractions. However, will is not just a principle of life negating everything, but it also makes suggestions for innovations, expands interests, changes priorities, deepens someone's personality. Led by one's will man acquires mind, which also humanizes his drives and emotions. A great deal of man's emotions is the consequence of efforts of one's will; e.g. meaning-happiness, i.e. happiness about the meaning of one's life.

Our knowledge of will, which has already been profound since the ancient world, was buried by Freudism; under its influence research on will disappeared after the Second World War. It has been revived since 1965 by the discovery of the brain potential that precedes voluntary movements which was found by a deliberate search for the cerebral bases of will: the Bereitschaftspotential that occurs in a mediofrontal localization. The method of "reverse averaging" of event-related potentials introduced by Kornhuber & Deecke in 1964 shows that when one learns under the effort of will, the success of learning correlates with the activation of the frontal cortex, and that—with the willful attempt to see something in your mind's eye (imagery)—the frontal cortex is activated first, and only thereafter the posterior areas of the brain are activated. Other experiments investigating action, in which attention has some significance, show the delegation of cerebral activity from initially frontal to parietal. The imaging methods, e.g. functional magnetic resonance imaging, fail to notice the leading role of the frontal cortex, because their time resolution is too low. Will is based on a distributed system of functions. Attention, which is a partial function of will, has two centers, the strategic one in the anterior cingulate gyrus, and the tactical one in the posterior parietal cortex. In the new research on will after the advent of the *Bereitschaftspotential* the idea of planning came up and with it the planning test of Shallice (Tower of London test), which is regarded as a functioning test for the frontal convexity. In Anglo-Saxon countries the discussion about will runs partly under the term of self- regulation, in the neurological literature under executive functions, which, however, is too narrow.

Upon personality psychology, so far, research on the will has hardly had any impact, although will is inherent in all five great personality factors, one has agreed on, e.g. in the factor conscientiousness, in the factor emotional control, etc. Twin research shows that individually specific influences on the development of someone's personality have an effect to a similar extent as the genome and a more extensive one than the shared environmental influences (i.e. shared with brothers and sisters). At the basis of these non-genetic, individually specific factors is above all the child's and adolescent's own will. This self-active development of man's personality leads to a great variety of individuals, which is much larger than the one of all animals. It is this abundance of differences, which makes the cooperation of people so fruitful.

The organ of will lies in the frontal brain, more precisely in the prefrontal cortex, which, however, for its leadership needs messages from the rest of the brain about the outer world and the inner world, about the needs, and from memory, etc. and it delegates tasks to other parts of the brain. There is a division of tasks in the frontal cortex, as Karl Kleist discovered by examining brain injured patients from the First World War, published in 1934: mental drive and productive thinking are represented in the dorsolateral and the polar prefrontal cortex, conscience and emotional control in the orbital cortex. The leadership on our thinking is assisted by the frontal working memory, which was discovered by Jacobsen in 1935. The frontomedial supplementary motor area (SMA), in which the Bereitschaftspotential prior to willful movements occurs, controls for the right moment to start a volitional movement.

The SMA works closely together with the basal ganglia, which assist the cortex (among others with motor tasks and with speaking) with the help of programmes learnt earlier.

The evolution of the creative and disciplining cortex of the will was, according to Kornhuber's theory, the decisive step to recent man (Homo sapiens sapiens), cultural man. This evolution was made possible by selection of will on the basis of cooperation. The evolution of speech obviously preceded the evolution of creativeness, probably as early as with Homo habilis two million years ago. Neanderthal man, who could certainly speak and even had 200 g more brain than Homo sapiens sapiens, lacked this creativeness, probably because he had a smaller frontal brain.

Creativeness, however, makes man dangerous for man and required the evolution of moral beyond the care of the brood; its substrate lies in the orbital brain, which is the youngest part of the cortex of will. The fact that man—thanks to his creative will—is a superior living being, results in duties that go far beyond him.

The limbic system in the further sense, the hypothalamus and certain brainstem nuclei, are old parts of the motivational system that are to a large extent anatomically unchanged in man as compared to the higher animals; the limbic system regulates drives and emotions for readiness for doing, nutrition, defense, reproduction, etc. which are still important for us but have been remolded by our reasoned will. Human feelings and drives are, however, by no means entirely elicited by the old motivational system but they are expanded and imprinted by culture and learning, the basis of which are the enormously enlarged association fields of the cerebral cortex (half of them being the cortex of will). Happiness of mind of the creative person for instance is initiated by willful action in the frontal cortex; it is experienced cortically, rests, however, upon the collaboration of subcortical regulators. It is an inner reward of meaningful volitional action and stabilizes the autonomy of the personality.

Will in the child matures later than the abilities of the senses, of the motor system and of speech, since the formation of the dendrites and synapses in the prefrontal cortex takes many years. The development, education, and self-education of will last all through youth into adulthood. The molding of the human personality has by no means been finished in early childhood. Therefore, the personality of a child or adolescent takes effect upon its own development. Will influences the formation of interests, the choice of friends, examples, etc., the acknowledgement of standards and the hierarchy of the values. Therefore, the differences in will and its world of values are much larger than the ones in the motor system or in intelligence. Above all, one's own activity is necessary, as for learning.

Youngsters, not yet firm in their will, are addressed by dealers and advertising with the goal of making them dependent. Addictions have now become worse than psychoses, since we have obtained efficient medicaments against the latter. Cigarettes and alcohol are the drugs most frequently used in Europe. Damages by alcohol (among others cancer, dementia and other brain damages) are still underestimated; they appear partly even prior to birth (due to women's alcoholism since 1968). Smoking during pregnancy is also detrimental to brain development.

Handicapped people can develop stern willpower. There is a humane nobility also with simple people, which is derived from long-term good will.

Freedom lies in will and its effect on thinking and acting. Positive freedom is natural, partial, relative. We must and can do something for it, partly by means of our own efforts and learning. The law expects from us a behavior supporting freedom. The prudence of human will enables the adult mentally healthy person to be responsible. Freedom of will is not against nature but an acquired ability of reasoned self-leadership. Total determinism contradicts itself. Freedom of will is neither chance nor arbitrariness, but rather the ability of choosing the good. The fact that freedom of will has a physical basis does not disprove it but makes it real.

Consciousness and the unconscious in the brain always cooperate. Information processing in the brain needs space, time and energy; it is based on collaboration in a distributed system but striving for unity under the leadership of ethical will.

Bibliography

Accenture-Studie. 2005. "Frauen suchen Vorbilder fürs Leben." *Frankfurt. Allg. Ztg.* March 5.
Ach, N. 1905. "Über die Willenstätigkeit und das Denken." Göttingen: Vandenhoek & Ruprecht.
Ach, N. 1910. "Über den Willensakt und das Temperament." Leipzig: Quelle & Meyer.
Ach, N. 1935. "Analyse des Willens." In: Handbuch der biologischen Arbeitsmethoden, ed. E. Abderhalden: Vol. 6., Berlin: Urban & Schwarzenberg.
Alexander, G.E., DeLong, M.R., Strick, P.L. 1986. "Parallel organisation of functionally segregated circuits linking basal ganglia and cortex." *Ann. Rev. Neurosci.* 9, 357–381.
Alexander, G.E., Crutcher, M.D., DeLong, M.R. 1990. "Basal ganglia-thalamocortical circuits: Parallel substrates for motor, oculomotor, 'prefrontal' and 'limbic' functions." In: *The prefrontal cortex.* Uylings, H.B.M. et al. eds., Amsterdam, New York, Oxford: Elsevier, 119–146.
Allport, G.W., Bruner, J.S., Jandorf, E.M. 1941. "Personality under social catastrophe." *Character and Personality.* 10, 1.
Amador, N., Fried, I. 2004. "Single-neuron activity in the human supplementary motor area underlying preparation for action." *J. Neurosurg.* 100, 250–259.
Amelang, M., Bartussek, D. 2001. "Differentielle Psychologie und Persönlichkeitsforschung." 5th Edition, Stuttgart: Kohlhammer.
Anderson, A.K., Phelps, E.A. 2002. "Is the human amygdala critical for subjective experience of emotion?" *J. Cognit. Neurosci.* 14, 709–720.
Anderson, S.W., Damasio, H., Tranel, D., Damasio, A.R. 2000. "Long term sequelae of prefrontal cortex damage acquired in early childhood." *Devel. Neuropsychol.* 18, 281–296.
Anderson, S.W., Damasio, A.R., Damasio, H. 2003. "A neural basis for collecting behavior in humans." *Society for Neuroscience. Abstract Viewer.* Abstract No. 195.9.

Anderson, V.A., Anderson, P., Northam, E., Jacobs, R., Mikiewicz, O. 2002. "Relationship between cognitive and behavioral measures of executive function in children with brain disease." *Child Neuropsychol.* 8, 231–240.

Anokhin, A.P., Heath, A.C., Ralano, A. 2003. "Genetic influences on frontal brain function: WCST performance in twins." *NeuroReport* 14. 1975–1978.

Aristoteles, 384–322 BC "Politik." Dt. Hamburg: Meiner.

Aristoteles, 384–322 BC, "Nikomachische Ethik." Deutsch bei Reclam.

Aristoteles, 384–322 BC, "Peri Psyches (De Anima)." Dt. Über die Seele. Hamburg: Meiner.

Arnstein, A.F.T., Robbins, T.W. 2002. "Neurochemical modulation of prefrontal cortical function in humans and animals." In: Stuss, D.T., Knight, R.T. eds.: *Principles of frontal lobe function.* New York, Oxford: University Press, 51–84.

Asch, S.E. 1951 "Effects of group pressure upon the modification and distortion of judgements." In: Guetzkow, H. ed. *Groups, leaderships and men.*, Pittsburgh, 177–190.

Asendorpf, J.B. 1999. "Psychologie der Persönlichkeit." 2nd Edition. Heidelberg: Springer.

Baldo, J.V., Delis, D., Kramer, J., Shimamura, A.P. 2002. "Memory performance on the California Verbal Learning Test—II: findings from patients with focal frontal lesions." *J. internat. neuropsychol. soc.* 8, 539–546.

Barbas, H., Pandya, D.N. 1991. "Patterns of connections of the prefrontal cortex in the rhesus monkey associated with cortical architecture." In: Levin, H.S., Eisenberg, H.M., Benton, H.L. eds.: *Frontal lobe function and dysfunction.*, New York, Oxford: Oxford University Press, 35–58.

Baumann, B., Bogerts, B. 1999. "The pathomorphology of schizophrenia and mood disorders: similarities and differences." *Schizophrenia Res.* 39, 141–148.

Beauregard, M., Levesque J., Bourgouin P. 2001. "Neural correlates of conscious self-regulation of emotion." *J. Neurosci 21, Rapid communications*, 165, 1–6.

Bechinger, D., Kongehl, G., Kornhuber, H.H. 1972. "Eine Hypothese für die physiologische Grundlage des Größensehens: Quantitative Untersuchungen der Informationsübertragung für Längen und Richtungen mit Punkten und Linien." *Arch. Psychiat. Nervenkr.* 215, 181–189.

Bechinger, D., Kornhuber, H.H., Schmidt, W. 1984. "Ein epidemiologischer Beweis für die Wirksamkeit der Frühbehandlung cerebraler Sprachstörungen mit Hilfe der Mütter." *Verh. Dtsch. Ges. Neurol.*, Vol. 3., Berlin, Heidelberg: Springer, 999–1002.

Bell, M., Bryson, G., Greig, T., Corcoran, C., Wexler, B.E. 2001. "Neurocognitive enhancement therapy with work therapy: effects on neuropsychological test performance." *Arch.gen. Psychiat.* 58, 763–768.

Benson, D.F. & Stuss, D.T. 1990. "Frontal lobe influences on delusions: a clinical perspective." *Schizophr. Bull.* 16, 403–411.

Berrios, G.E., Gili, M. 1995. "Will and its disorders: a conceptual history." *History of Psychiat.* 6, 87–104.

Berthier, M.L., Kulisevsky J.J., Gironell, A., Lopes, O.L. 2001. "Obsessive-compulsive disorder and traumatic brain injury: behavioral, cognitive, and neuroimaging findings." *Neuropsychiat., Neuropsychol. & Behavioral Neurology* 14, 23–31.

Bieri, P. 2001. "Das Handwerk der Freiheit. Über die Entdeckung des eigenen Willens." Munich: Hanser.
Binder, W., Kornhuber, H.H., Waiblinger, G. 1984. "Benzodiazepinsucht, unsere iatrogene Seuche—157 Fälle von Benzodiazepin-Abhängigkeit." *Öff. Gesund.-wes.* 46, 80–86.
Birnboim, S. 2003. "The automatic and controlled information-processing dissociation: is it still relevant?" *Neuropsychol. Rev.* 13. 19–31.
Bleich, S. et al. 2001. "Moderate alcohol consumption in social drinkers raises plasma homocysteine levels: a contradiction to the "French paradox"?" *Alcoh. & Alcoholism.* 36, 189–192.
Boden, G., Chen, X., De Santis, A., Kendrick, Z. 1993. "Ethanol inhibits insulin action on lipolysis and on insulin in elderly men." *Amer. J. Physiol. Endocr. Metabol.* 265, E197–E202.
Breitenseher, M., Uhl, F., Prayer-Wimberger, D., Deecke, L., Trattnig, S., Kramer, J. 1998. "Morphological dissociation between visual pathways and cortex: MRI of visual deprived patients with congenital peripheral blindness." *Neuroradiology* 40, 424–427.
Brezinka, W. 1987. "Tüchtigkeit. Analyse und Bewertung eines Erziehungszieles." Munich, Basel: Reinhardt.
Brierley, B., Shaw, P., David, A.S. 2002. "The human amygdala: a systematic review and meta-analysis of volumetric magnetic resonance imaging." *Brain Res. Rev.* 39, 84–105.
Brugger, P., Monsch, A.U., Salmon, D.P., Butters, N. 1996. "Random number generation in dementia of the Alzheimer type: a test of frontal executive functions." *Neuropsychologia* 34, 97–103.
Brunner, R.J., Kornhuber, H.H., Seemüller, E., Suger, G., Wallesch, C.W. 1982. "Basal ganglia participation in language pathology." *Brain and Language* 16, 281–299.
Bruno, Giordano. 1548–1600. "Ges. Werke." Leipzig 1904–1909.
Buckner, R.L., Kelley, W.M., Pettersen, S.E. 1999. "Frontal cortex contributes to human memory formation." *Nature Neurosci.* 1, 211–314.
Bühler, Ch. 1959. "Der menschliche Lebenslauf als psychologisches Problem." Göttingen: Verl. f. Psychologie Hogrefe.
Bühler, K. 1929. "Die Krisis der Psychologie." 2nd Edition. Jena.
Bunge, M. 1979. "Treatise on basic philosophy." Vol. 14, Ontology II: A world of systems. Dordrecht, Boston, London: Reidel.
Burton, H., Sinclair, R.J. 2000. "Attending to and remembering tactile stimuli: a review of brain imaging data and single neuron responses." *J. clin. Neurophysiology* 17, 575–591.
Campbell, B.G. 1970. "Human evolution, an introduction to man's adaptation." 4th Edition. Chicago: ALDINE Publ. Comp.
Catafau, A.M., Parellada, E., Lomena, F. et al. 1998. "Role of the cingulate gyrus during the Wisconsin Card Sorting Test: a single photon emission computed tomography study in normal volonteers." *Psychiat. Res.* 83, 67–74.
CDBE Europ. Council on Disorders of the Brain. 2005. "Executive summary." *Eur. J. Neur. Suppl.* 1.

Conrad, B., Kornhuber, H.H. 1967. "Zur bilateralen sensorischen Integration beim Menschen: Die Wahrnehmung der Gleichzeitigkeit von rechts- und linksseitigen somatosensiblen und visuellen Reizen bei Gesunden und Kranken mit Großhirnläsionen." *Pflügers Arch. Physiol.* 294, R60–R61.

Conway, M.A., Fthenaki, A. 2003. "Disruption of inhibitory control of memory following lesions to the frontal and temporal lobes." *Cortex* 39, 667–686.

Coolidge, F.L., Griego, J.A. 1995. "Executive functions of the frontal lobes: psychometric properties of a self-rating scale." *Psychol. Report* 77, 24–26.

Cornfeld, G. ed. 1969. "Die Bibel und ihre Welt." Bergisch Gladbach: Lübbe.

Coulmas, F. 2005. "Hiroshima. Geschichte und Nachgeschichte." Munich: Beck.

Creutzfeldt, O.D. 1995. "Cortex cerebri, performance, structured and functional organisation of the cortex," translated by Mary Creutzfeldt. Oxford Univ. Press.

Cummings, J.L., Frankel, M. 1985. "Gilles de la Tourette Syndrome and the neurological basis of obsessions and compulsions." *Biol. Psychiat.* 20, 1117–1126.

Cunnington, R., Windischberger, C., Deecke, L., Moser, C. 1999. "The use of single event fMRI and fuzzy clustering analysis to examine haemodynamic response time courses in supplementary motor and primary motor cortical areas." *Biomed. Technik* 44, Suppl. 2, 116–119.

Cunnington, R., Windischberger, C., Deecke, L., Moser, C. 2002. "The preparation and execution of selfinitiated and externally triggered movement: a study of event-related fMRI." *Neuroimage* 15, 373–385.

Current Contents Life Sciences. 1990. Citation Classic: "Readiness for movement—the Bereitschaftspotential story." 33, 14.

Cusanus, Nikolaus. 1488. "Opera." Deutsch. Hrsg. Heidelberger Akad. Wiss. 1932ff.

Czikszentmihalyi, M. 1992. "Flow, das Geheimnis des Glücks." Stuttgart: Klett-Cotta.

Czikszentmihalyi, M. 1997. "Kreativität. Stuttgart: Klett-Cotta."

Danek, A., Göhringer, T. 2005. "Kognitive Neurologie und Neurobiologie." In: Förstl, H. ed.: Frontalhirn. Funktionen und Grundlagen. 2nd Edition. Heidelberg: Springer Medizin Verlag, 41–82.

Darwin, Ch. 1871. "The descent of man, and selection in relation to sex." London.

Deci, E.L., 1980. "The psychology of self-determinism." Free Press.

Deci, E.L., Ryan, R.M. 1985. "Intrinsic motivation and self-determination of human behavior." New York, Plenum Press.

Deci, E.L., Ryan, R.M. 2004. "Handbook of Self-determination research." Boydell & Brewer.

Deecke, L., Kornhuber, H.H. 1978. "An electrical sign of participation of the mesial supplementary" motor cortex in human voluntary finger movement." *Brain Res.* 159, 473–476.

Deecke, L., Heise, B., Kornhuber, H.H., Lang, M., Lang W. 1984. "Brain potentials associated with voluntary manual tracking: Bereitschaftspotential, conditioned premotion positivity, directed attention potential, and relaxation potential." Anticipatory activity of the limbic and frontal cortex. In: Karrer, R., Cohen, J., Tueting, P. eds.: Ann. N.Y. Acad. Sci. 425. 450–464.

Deecke, L., Scheid, P., Kornhuber, H.H. 1969. "Distribution of readiness potential, pre-motion positivity and motion potential of the human cerebral cortex preceding voluntary finger movements." *Exp. Brain Res.* 7, 158–168.

Deecke, L., Grözinger, B., Kornhuber, H.H. 1976. "Voluntary finger movement in man: Cerebral potentials and theory." *Biol Cybern* 23, 99–119.
Deecke, L., Kornhuber, H.H. 2003. "Human freedom, reasoned will, and the brain: the Bereitschaftspotential story." In: Jahanshahi, M., Hallet, M. eds.: The Bereitschaftspotential. New York: Kluwer Academic/Plenum Publ. 283–320.
Delacour, J. 1997. "Neurobiology of consciousness: an overview." *Behav. Brain Res.* 85, 127–141.
Democritus, about 500 BC, In Diels, H., Kranz, W. eds.: Die Fragmente der Vorsokratiker. 18th Edition. 1989, Zürich: Weidmanns.
Dennett, D. 2003. "Freedom evolves." Cambridge Mass.: MIT Press.
Dennett, D. 2005. "Sweet Dreams. Philosophical obstacles to a science of consciousness." Cambridge Mass.: MIT Press.
Descartes, R. 1644. "Principia philosophiae." Amsterdam: Dt. Philos. Bibl. 28. Hamburg: Meiner 1965.
DeVries, G.J., Miller, M.A. 1998. "Anatomy and function of extrahypothalamic vasopressin systems in the brain." *Progr. Brain Res.* 119, 3–20.
Dilthey, W. 1894. "Ideen über eine beschreibende und zergliedernde Psychologie." In: Misch, G. ed. 1982. Gesammelte Schriften. Vol. V.
Dostojewski, F.M., without year, "Memoiren aus einem Totenhaus." Leipzig: Moser.
Dronkers, N.F., Wilkins, D.P., VanValin, R.D. jr., Redfern, B.B., Jaeger, J.J. 2004. "Lesion analysis of the brain areas involved in language comprehension." *Cognition* 92, 145–177.
Dunant, J.H. 1942., Erinnerungen an Solferino und andere Dokumente zur Gründung des Roten Kreuzes." Zürich: Atlantis.
Erasmus von Rotterdam, D. 1524. "De libero arbitrio diatribe sive collatio." Dt. Vom freien Willen. Ausgew. Schriften Vol. VI. 1969.
Eccles, J.C., Zeier, H. 1980."Gehirn und Geist." Zürich: Kindler.
Elf führende Neurowissenschaftler. 2004. "Das Manifest. Über Gegenwart und Zukunft der Hirnforschung." Gehirn und Geist 6, 30–37.
Emery, N.J., Capitanio, J.P., Mason, W.A., Machado, C.J., Mendoza, S.P., Amaral, D.G. 2001. "The effect of bilateral lesions of the amygdala on dyadic social interactions in rhesus monkeys, Macaca mulata." *Behav. Neurosci.* 115, 515–544.
Ernst, C, von Luckner, N. 1985. "Stellt die Frühkindheit die Weichen? Eine Kritik an der Lehre von der schicksalhaften Bedeutung erster Erlebnisse." Stuttgart: Enke.
Espy, K.A., Kaufmann, P.M., McDiarmid, M.D., Glisky, M.L. 1999. "Executive functioning in preschool children: Performance on A-Not-B and other delayed response format tasks." *Brain and Cognition* 41, 178–199.
Eslinger, P.J., Grattan, E.L., Damasio, H., Damasio, A.R. 1992. "Developmental consequences of childhood frontal lobe damage." *Arch. Neurol.* 49, 764–769.
Evans, D.A., Hebert, L.E., Beckett, C.A. et al. 1997. "Education and other measures of socioeconomic status and risk of incident Alzheimer disease in a defined population of older persons." *Arch. Neurol.* 54, 1399–1404.
Farrow, T.F., Zheng, Y., Wilkinson, I.D. et al. 2001. "Investigating the functional anatomy of empathy and forgiveness." *Neuroreport* 12, 2433–2438.
Federalist, The. 1788. "Papers of Alexander Hamilton, James Madison & John Jay." New York.

Fichte, J.G. 1808. "Reden an die deutsche Nation." Sämtliche Werke. 2nd Edition., 1845, Vol. 7, 281.

Filley, C.M. et al. 2001. "Toward an understanding of violence: neurobehavioral aspects of unwarranted physical aggression: Aspen neurobehavioral conference consensus statement." *Neuropsychiat. Neuropsychol. & Behavioral Neurol.* 14, 1–14.

Fischer, R.S., Alexander, M.P., D'Esposito, M., Otto, R. 1995. "Neuropsychological and neuroanatomical correlates of confabulation." *J. clin. exp. Neuropsychol.* 17. 20–28.

Flashman, L.A. 2002. "Disorders of awareness in neuropsychiatric syndromes: an update." *Current Psychiatry Reports* 4, 346–353.

Fletcher, P.C., Henson, R.N. 2001. "Frontal lobes and human memory: insights from functional neuroimaging." *Brain* 124, 849–889.

Frankl, V.E. 1986. "The Doctor and the Soul. From Psychotherapy to Logotherapy." Souvenir Press, London.

Frankl, V.E. 1988. "The Will to Meaning: Foundations and Applications of Logotherapy." New York, New American Library.

Frankl, V.E. 1997. "Man's Search for Ultimate Meaning." New York, Perseus Book Publishing.

Franziscus of Assisi see Goez, W.

Fratiglioni, L., Ahlbom, A., Vittanen, M. et al. 1993. "Risk factors for late-onset Alzheimer's disease: a population based, case-control study." *Ann. Neurol.* 33, 258–266.

Freeman, W.J., Watts, J.W. 1942. Psychosurgery: "Intelligence, emotion and social behavior following prefrontal lobotomy for mental disorders." Springfield: Thomas.

Fuster, J.M. 1990. "Behavioral electrophysiology of the prefrontal cortex of the primate." In: Uylings, H.B.M. et al. eds.: *The prefrontal cortex*. Amsterdam, New York, Oxford: Elsevier. 313–324.

Fuster, J.M. 1991. "Role of prefrontal cortex in delay tasks: evidence from reversible lesion and unit recording in the monkey." In: Levin, H.S., Eisenberg, H.M., Benton, H.L., Hgg.: Frontal lobe function and dysfunction. New York, Oxford: Oxford University Press. 59–78.

Fuster, J.M. 1999. "Synopsis of function and dysfunction of the frontal lobe." *Acta Psychiat. Scand. Suppl.* 395, 51–57.

Garden, S.E., Phillips, L.H., MacPherson, S.E. 2001. "Midlife aging, open ended planning and laboratory measures of executive function." *Neuropsychology* 15, 472–482.

Gautama, Buddha, s. Buddhismus in H. von Glasenapp. 1963. *Die fünf Weltreligionen*. Munich: Diederichs.

Gaykema, R.P., van Weeghel, R., Hersh, L.B., Luiten, P.G. 1991. "Prefrontal cortical projections to the cholinergic neurons in the basal forebrain." *J. comp. Neur.* 303, 563–583.

Gerloff, C., Corwell, B., Chen, R., Hallet, M., Cohen, L.G. 1999. "Stimulation over the human supplementary motor area interferes with the organisation of future elements in complex motor sequences." *Brain* 120. 1587–1602.

Global Marshall Plan Initiative. 2005. "Impulse für eine Welt in Balance." Hamburg: Global Marshall Plan Foundation.

Goel, V., Grafman, J., Sadato, N., Hallett M. 1995. "Modelling other minds." *NeuroReport* 6, 1741–1746.
Goethe, J.W. von. 1796. "Wilhelm Meister's Apprenticeship Vol. XIV Harvard Classics Shelf of Fiction. New York. Bartleby.com, 2000.
Goez, W. 1983. Franziscus von Assisi. In: *Goez, W.: Gestalten des Hochmittelalters.* Darmstadt: Wiss. Buchgesellschaft. 315–330.
Goldberg, G., Bloom, K.K. 1990. "The alien hand sign. Localisation, lateralisation and recovery." *Am. J. Phys. Med. & Rehabil.* 69, 228–238.
Goldin-Meadow, S., Feldman, H. 1977. "The development of language-like communication without a language model." *Science* 197, 401–403.
Goldman-Rakic, P.S. 1987. "Development of cortical circuitry and cognitive function." *Child Developm.* 58, 601–622.
Goldman-Rakic, P.S. 1990. "Cellular and circuit basis of working memory in prefrontal cortex of nonhuman primates." In: Uylings, H.B.M. et al. eds.: The prefrontal cortex. Amsterdam, New York, Oxford: Elsevier, 325–336.
Gollwitzer P. 1970. "Abwägen und Planen." Göttingen, Hogrefe.
Goschke, Th. 1996. Wille und Kognition. Zur funktionalen Architektur der intentionalen Handlungssteuerung pp. 583–663. In: J. Kuhl, H. Heckhausen eds. Enzyklopädie der Psychologie. Vol. Motivation, Volition und Handlung. Göttingen, Hogrefe.
Grandjean, D., Sander, D., Pourtois, G. et al. 2005. "The voices of wrath: brain responses to angry prosody in meaningless speech." *Nature Neurosc.* 8, 145–146.
Grotius, H. 1625. "De iure belli ac pacis libri tres." Paris.
Gruber, O., Arendt, T., von Cramon, D.Y. 2005. "Neurobiologische Grundlagen." In: Förstl, H. ed. Frontalhirn. Funktionen und Grundlagen. 2nd Edition. Heidelberg: Springer Medizin Verlag, 15–40.
Haggard, P. 2008. "Human volition: towards a neuroscience of will." *Nature Rev. Neuroscience* 9, 934–946.
Haier, R.J., Jung, R.E., Yeo, R.A., Head, K., Alkire, M.T. 2004. "Structural brain variation and general intelligence." *NeuroImage* 23, 425–433.
Halder, G., Callaerts, P., Gehring, W.J. 1995. "Induction of ectopic eyes by targeted expression of the eyeless gene in Drosophila." *Science* 267, 1788–1792.
Hartmann, N. 1953. "New ways of ontology." Chicago. H. Regnery Co. c1952.
Hartmann, N. 1951. "Teleologisches Denken." Berlin: De Gruyter.
Heckhausen, H. 1987. "Perspektiven einer Psychologie des Wollens." In: *Heckhausen, H., Gollwitzer, P.M., Weinert, F.E.* eds.: Jenseits des Rubikon: Der Wille in den Humanwissenschaften. Berlin, Heidelberg: Springer-Verlag. 121–142.
Hegel, G. F. W. 1821. "Grundlinien der Philosophie des Rechts." Berlin: Nicolai. Phil. Bibl. 4th Edition. 1955. Hamburg: Meiner.
Heimer, L. 2003. "A new anatomical framework for neuropsychiatric disorders and drug abuse."*Am. J. Psychiat.* 160, 1726–1739.
Heinroth, J.C.A. 1818. "Lehrbuch der Störungen des Seelenlebens." 1. Teil. S. 347. Leipzig: Vogel.
Held, R., Hein, A. 1963. "Movement-produced stimulation in the development of visually guided behaviour." *J. Comp. Physiol. Psychol.* 56, 872–876.

Hellbrügge, Th. ed. 1981. "Klinische Sozialpädiatrie." Berlin: Springer.
Heraclitus, about 500 BC. "Fragmente." In: Diels, H., Kranz, W. eds.: *Die Fragmente der Vorsokratiker.* 18th Edition. 1989. Zürich: Weidmann.
Hershberger, W. ed. 1989. "Volitional Action. Conation and Control." Amsterdam, New York: North-Holland.
Hess, W.R. 1949. "Das Zwischenhirn. Syndrome, Lokalisationen, Funktionen." Basel: Schwabe.
Heston, L.L., Denny, D.D., Pauley, I.B. 1966. "The adult adjustment of persons institutionalized as children." *Brit. J. Psychiatry* 112, 1103–1110.
Hetzer, H. 1987. "Zur Psychologie des Kindes." Darmstadt: Wiss. Buchgesellschaft.
Hinkle, L.E., Wolff, H.G. 1957. "The Methods of interrogation and indoctrination used by the communist state police." *Bull. N. Y.Acad. Med.* 33, 600–615.
Holloway, R.L. 1983. "Human paleontological evidence relevant to language behavior." Hum. Neurobiol. 2, 3, 105–114.
Howard, G.S., Myers, P.R. 1989. "Some experimental investigations of volition." In: Hershberger, W.A. ed.: *Volitional Action.* Amsterdam, New York: North Holland. 335–352.
Iacoboni, M., Molnar-Szakacz, I., Gallese, V., Buccino, G., Mazziotta, J.C., Rizzolatti, G. 2005. "Grasping the intentions of others with one's own mirror neuron system." *PloS. Biol.* 3, e 79, 1–20.
Ihara, H., Berrios, G.E., London, M. 2000. "Group and case study of the dysexecutive syndrome in alcoholism without amnesia." *J. Neurol. Neurosurg. & Psychiat.* 68, 731–737.
Ingvar, D. 1994. "The will of the brain: cerebral correlates of willful acts." *J. theor. Biol.* 171, 7–12.
Jacobs, R., Anderson, V. 2002. "Planning and problem solving skills following focal frontal brain lesions in childhood: analysis using the tower of London." *Child Neuropsychol.* 8, 93–106.
Jacobsen, C.F. 1935. "Functions of the frontal association area in primates." *Arch. Neurol. Psychiat.* 33, 558–569.
Jacobsen, C.F. 1936. "Studies of cerebral functions in primates. 1. The functions of frontal association areas in monkeys." *Comp. Psychol. Monographs* 13, 3–60.
Jahanshahi, M., Hallet, M. eds. 2003. "The Bereitschaftspotential. Movement-related cortical potentials." New York: Kluwer Plenum.
James, William. 1890. "The Principles of Psychology." New York: Holt.
Janzarik, W. 1993. "Steuerung und Entscheidung, deviante Strukturierung und Selbstkorrumpierung im Vorfeld affektiv akzentuierter Delikte." In: *Saß, H.* ed.: Affektdelikte – Interdisziplinäre Beiträge zur Beurteilung von affektiv akzentuierten Straftaten. Berlin, Heidelberg, New York: Springer.
Janzarik, W. 2000. "Handlungsanalyse und forensische Bewertung seelischer Devianz." *Nervenarzt* 71, 181–187.
Jaspers, K. 1919. "Psychologie der Weltanschauungen." Berlin: Springer.
Jaspers, K. 1936. "Nietzsche." Berlin, De Gruyter.
Jaspers, K. 1946. "Allgemeine Psychopathologie, Neufassung." Berlin, Heidelberg: Springer.

Jaspers, K. 1951. "Solon." In: Jaspers, K: *Rechenschaft und Ausblick.* Munich: Piper.
Jaspers, K. 1958. "Von der Wahrheit." Munich: Piper.
Jaspers, K. 1977. "Was ist Erziehung?" Munich: Piper.
Jessen, P.W.C. 1847. "Über die in Beziehung auf Geistes- und Gemütskranke herrschenden Vorurteile." *Allg. Z. Psychiat.* 4, 1–8.
Jones-Gutman, M., Milner, D. 1977. "Design fluency. The invention of non-sense drawings after focal cortical lesions." *Neuropsychologia* 15, 653–674.
Jones, E.G., Powell, T.P.S. 1970. "An anatomical study of converging sensory pathways within the cerebral cortex of the monkey." *Brain* 93, 793–820.
Kane, R. ed. 2002. "The Oxford Handbook of Free Will." New York: Oxford University Press.
Kanfer, F.H., Koroly, P. 1972. "Self-control: a behavioristic excursion into the lions den." Behavior Therapy 3: 398–416.
Kanfer, F.H. 1977. "Self-regulation and self-control." In: H. Zeier, Ed., *Die Psychologie des XX. Jahrhunderts.* Vol. 4, pp. 793–827. Zürich, Kindler.
Kanfer, F.H. 1979. "Self-management: Strategies and tactics. Maximizing treatment gains." Academic Press.
Kanfer, F.H. 1986. "Selbst-Regulation und Verhalten." In: Heckhausen et al. eds.: *Jenseits des Rubikon.* Heidelberg, Springer pp. 286–299.
Kant, I. 1785. "Grundlegung zur Metaphysik der Sitten." Riga: Hartknoch.
Kant, I. 1795. "Zum ewigen Frieden." Königsberg: Nicolovius.
Kawamura, K. 1977. "Cortico-cortical fiber connections of the cortical „association" areas of cats, monkeys and man." *Advance in Neurol. Sci. Japan* 21, 1085–1101 and. 1973. *Brain Res.* 51, 23–40.
Kierkegaard, S. 1846. "Abschließende unwissenschaftliche Nachschrift, zu den philosophischen Brocken." Dt. In: Ges. Werke. 190–1922. Jena: Diederichs.
King, A.C., Taylor, C.B., Haskel, W.L., DeBusk, R.F. 1989. "Influence of regular aerobic exercise on psychological health." *Health Psychol.* 8, 305–324.
Kleist, K. 1934. "Kriegsverletzungen des Gehirns in ihrer Bedeutung für die Hirnlokalisation und Hirnpathologie." Leipzig: Barth.
Knight, R.T., Nakada, T. 1998. "Cortico-limbic circuits and novelty: a review of EEG and blood flow data." *Reviews in the Neurosci.* 9, 57–70.
Knight, R.T., Stuss, D.T. 2002. "Prefrontal cortex: the present and the future." In: Stuss, D.T., Knight, R.T. eds.: *Principles of frontal lobe function.* New York: Oxford. 573–595.
Kohler, I. 1951. "Über Aufbau und Wandlungen der Wahrnehmungswelt." *Sitzungsber. Österr. Akad. Wiss. philos.-histor. Klasse.* 377, 1–118.
Kornhuber, H.H. 1955. "Über Auslösung zyklothymer Depressionen durch seelische Erschütterungen." *Arch. Psychiat. Nervenkr.* 193, 391–405.
Kornhuber, H.H. 1961. "Psychologie und Psychiatrie der Kriegsgefangenschaft." In: Gruhle, H.W., Jung, R., Mayer-Gross, W., Müller, M. eds.: *Psychiatrie der Gegenwart.* Vol. III. Berlin, Göttingen, Heidelberg: Springer. 631–742.
Kornhuber, H.H. 1962. "Zur Situationsabhängigkeit von Bedürfnissen und Neurosen nach Erfahrungen in Gefangenenlagern." In: Krantz, H. ed.: *Psychopathologie heute. Festschrift für Kurt Schneider.* Stuttgart: Thieme. 252–257.

Kornhuber, H.H. 1965. "Zur Bedeutung multisensorischer Integration im Nervensystem." Dtsch. Zschr. F. Nervenkrankh. 187, 478–484.

Kornhuber, H.H. 1972. "Tastsinn und Lagesinn." In: Gauer, O.H., Kramer, K., Jung, R. eds.: *Physiologie des Menschen.* Vol. 11. Munich, Berlin, Vienna: Urban & Schwarzenberg. 51–112.

Kornhuber, H.H. 1973. "Neural control of input into longterm memory: limbic system and amnestic syndrome in man." In: Zippel, H.P. ed.: *Memory and transfer of information.* New York: Plenum Press.

Kornhuber, H.H. 1974. "Cerebral cortex, cerebellum and basal gangalia: an introduction to their motor functions." In: Schmitt, F.U., Worden, F.G. eds.: *The Neurosciences. Third Study Program.* Cambridge Mass.: MIT Press. 267–280.

Kornhuber, H.H. 1977. "A reconsideration of the cortical and subcortical mechanisms involved in speech and Aphasia." In: Desmedt, J.E. ed.: *Progr. Clin. Neurophysiol.* Vol. 3, Basel: Karger. 28–35.

Kornhuber, H.H. 1978. "Zur Situation der Familie." *Der Kinderarzt* 9, 1319–1325.

Kornhuber, H.H. 1978a. "Geist und Freiheit als biologische Probleme." In: *Stamm, R.A., Zeier, H.* eds.: *Die Psychologie des 20. Jahrhunderts.* Vol. VI, Zürich: Kindler. 1122–1130.

Kornhuber, H.H. 1978b. "Wahrnehmung und Informationsverarbeitung." In: Stamm, R.A., Zeier, H., eds. *Die Psychologie des 20. Jahrhunderts.* Bd. VI. Zürich: Kindler. 783–798.

Kornhuber, H.H. 1978c. "Motorische Systeme und sensomotorische Integration." In: Stamm, R.A., Zeier, H. eds.: *Die Psychologie des 20. Jahrhunderts.* Bd. VI. Zürich: Kindler. 750–762.

Kornhuber, H.H. 1982. "Primärprävention des Zigarettenrauchens." In: *Rauchen oder Gesundheit.* Hamburg: Neuland Verlag. 126–133.

Kornhuber, H.H. 1984. "Von der Freiheit." In: Lindauer, M., Schöpf, A. eds.: *Wie erkennt der Mensch die Welt?* Stuttgart: Klett. 83–112.

Kornhuber, H.H. 1984a. "Attention, readiness for action, and the stages of voluntary decision." *Exp. Brain Res. Suppl.* 9, 420–429.

Kornhuber, H.H. 1984b. "Neue Ansätze zu einer Theorie des Traumschlafs." *Nervenarzt* 55, 54.

Kornhuber, H.H. 1987. "Handlungsentschluß, Aufmerksamkeit und Lernmotivation im Spiegel menschlicher Hirnpotentiale, mit Bemerkungen zu Wille und Freiheit." In: Heckhausen, H., Gollwitzer, P.M., Weinert, F.E. eds.: *Jenseits des Rubikon: Der Wille in den Humanwissenschaften.* Berlin, Heidelberg: Springer. 376–401.

Kornhuber, H.H. 1988. "The human brain: from dream and cognition to fantasy, will, conscience, and freedom." In: Markowitsch, H.J. ed.: *Information processing by the brain.* Toronto, Bern, Stuttgart: Hans Huber Publ. 241–258.

Kornhuber, H.H. 1988a. "Das Risiko Benzodiazepin." *Dt. Ärztebl.* 85, A 536, A 2091.

Kornhuber, H.H. 1992. "Gehirn, Wille, Freiheit." *Rev. Metaphys. et Morale.* 2. 203–223.

Kornhuber, H.H. 1993. "Prefrontal cortex and Homo sapiens: on creativity and reasoned will." *Neurol. Psychiat. Brain Res* 2, 1–6.

Kornhuber, H.H. 1995. "Präfrontalcortex-Funktion und Homo sapiens." In: Lang, W., Deecke, L., Hopf, H.C. eds. Verh. Dtsch. Ges. Neurol. 9, 40–48.

Kornhuber, H.H. 2001. "Alkohol, auch der normale Konsum schadet." Munich: Urban & Vogel.

Kornhuber, H.H. 2004. "Prävention von Demenz, einschließlich der Alzheimer-Krankheit." *Gesundh. Wes.* 66, 346–351.

Kornhuber, H.H., Bechinger, D., Jung, H., Sauer, E. 1985. "A quantitative relationship between the extent of localized cerebral lesions and the intellectual and behavioral deficiency in children." *Eur. Arch. Psychiat. Neurol. Sci.* 235, 129–133.

Kornhuber, H.H., Deecke, L. 1964. "Hirnpotentialänderungen beim Menschen vor und nach Willkürbewegungen und passiven Bewegungen des Menschen, dargestellt mit Magnetbandspeicherung und Rückwärtsanalyse." *Pflügers Arch. Physiol.* 281, 52.

Kornhuber, H.H., Deecke, L. 1965. "Hirnpotentialänderungen bei Willkürbewegungen und passiven Bewegungen des Menschen: Bereitschaftspotential und reafferente Potentiale." *Pflügers Arch. Physiol.* 284, 1–17.

Kornhuber, H.H., Deecke, L., Lang, W., Lang, M., Kornhuber, A. 1989. "Will, volitional action, attention and cerebral potentials in man: Bereitschaftspotential, performance related potentials, directed attention potential. EEG-spectrum changes." In: Hershberger, W.A. ed.: *Volitional action.* Amsterdam: Elsevier. 107–168.

Kornhuber, H.H., Füchtner, J. 1992. "More than tenfold increase of alcoholism in women since 1968." *Neurol. Psychiat. Brain Res.* 1, 46–48.

Kornhuber, H.H., Schütz, A. 1990. "Efficient treatment of neurogenic bladder in multiple sclerosis with initial intermittend catheterization and ultrasound-controlled training." *Europ. Neurol.* 30, 260–267.

Kosfeld, M., Heinrichs, M., Zak, P.J., Fischbacher, U. & Fehr, E. 2005. "Ocytocin increases trust in humans." *Nature* 435/2, 673–676.

Kotima, A.J., Moilanen, I., Taanila, A., Ebeling, H., Smalley, S.L., McGouch, J.J., Hartikainen, A.L., Jaervelin, M.R. 2003. "Maternal smoking and hyperactivity in 8–year old children." *J. Amer. Acad. Child Adolesc. Psychiat.* 42, 826–833.

Kropotkin, P.A. 1902. "Mutual aid." London. Dt. 1904. *Gegenseitige Hilfe in der Entwicklung.* Leipzig: Thomas.

Kuhl, J. 1986. "Motivation und Handlungskontrolle: Ohne guten Willen geht es nicht." In: H. Heckhausen, P.M. Gollwitzer, F.E. Weinert eds.: *Jenseits des Rubikon.* Heidelberg, Springer, pp. 101–120.

Kuhl, J. 1994. "A theory of action and state orientation." In: J. Kuhl & J. Beckmann, Eds. *Volition and personality: action and state orientation.* Göttingen, Hogrefe.

Kuhl, J. 1996. "Wille und Freiheitserleben: Formen der Selbststeuerung." In: Enzyklopädie der Psychologie, Vol. Motivation. Göttingen, Vandenhoeck & Ruprecht, pp. 665–765.

Kungtse, about 500 BC, Lun-yü. Gespräche. 1955. translated by V. R. Wilhelm. Munich: Diederich. 1989. translated by v. Bock, K. Kettwig: Phaidon.

Kwon, J.S., Kim, J.J., Lee, D.W. et al. 2003. "Neural correlates of clinical symptoms and cognitive dysfunctions in obsessive compulsive disorder." *Psychiat. Res.* 122, 37–47.

Lang, W., Lang, M., Kornhuber, A., Deecke, L., Kornhuber, H.H. 1983. "Human cerebral potentials and visuomotor learning." *Pflügers Archiv. Eur. J. Physiol.* 399, 342–344.

Lang, W., Lang, M., Heise, B., Deecke, L., Kornhuber, H.H. 1984. "Brain potentials related to voluntary hand tracking, motivation and attention." *Hum Neurobiol* 3: 235–240.

Lang, W., Lang, M., Kornhuber, A., Kornhuber, H.H. 1986. "Electrophysiological evidence for right frontal lobe dominance in spatial visuo-motor learning." *Arch. Ital. Biol.* 124, 1–13.

Lang, M., Lang, W., Uhl, F., Kornhuber, A. 1989. "Patterns of event related potentials in paired associative learning tasks: Learning and directed attention." In: *Maurer, K.* ed.: Topographic brain mapping in EEG and evoked potentials. Heidelberg: Springer. 323–325.

Lashley, K.S. 1931. "Mass action in cerebral function." *Science* 73: 245–254.

Lee, A.C., Robbins, T.W., Smith, S., Calvert, G.A., Tracey, I., Matthews, P., Owen, A.M. 2002. "Evidence for asymmetric frontal-lobe involvement in episodic memory from functional magnetic resonance imaging and patients with unilateral frontal-lobe excisions." *Neuropsychologia* 40, 2420–2437.

Lee, M., Vaughn, B.E., Kopp, C.B. 1983. "Role of self-control in the performance of very young children on a delayed-response memory-for-location task." *Devel. Psychol.* 19, 40–44.

Lengfelder, A., Gollwitzer, P.M. 2001. "Reflective and reflexive action control in patients with frontal brain lesion." *Neuropsychologia* 15, 80–100.

Lenski, G. 1970. "Human societies. A macrolevel introduction to sociology." New York.

Leon, D.A., Chenet, L., Shkolnikov, V.H., Zakharov, S., Shapiro, J., Rakhmanova, G., Vassin, S., McKee, M. 1997. "Huge variation in Russian mortality rates 1984–1994: Artefact, alcohol, or what? *Lancet* 350, 383–388.

Leubuscher. 1847. "Über Abulie." *Zeitschr. für Psychiat.* 4, 562–578.

Levin, H.S., Culhane, K.A., Hartmann, J., Evankovich, K., Mattson, A.J., Harward, A., Ringholz, B. Ewing-Cobbs, L., Fletcher, J.M. 1991. "Developmental changes in performance on tests on purported frontal lobe functioning." *Dev. Neuropsychol.* 7, 377–395.

Levine, B., Robertson, I.H., Clare, L., Carter, G., Hong, J., Wilson, B.A., Duncan, J., Stuss, D.T. 2000. "Rehabilitation of executive functioning: an experimental-clinical validation of goal management training." *J. Internat. Neuropsychol. Soc.* 6, 299–312.

Lewin, K. 1926. "Vorsatz, Wille und Bedürfnis." *Psychol. Forschung* 7, 330–385.

Leynes, P.A:, Marsh, R.L., Allen, J.D., Mayhorn, C.B. 2003. "Investigating the encoding and retrieval of intentions with event-related potentials." *Consciousness & Cognition* 12, 1–18.

Libet, B., Gleason, C.A., Wright, E.W., Pearl, D.K. 1983. "Time of conscious intention to act in relation to onset of cerebral activity, readiness potential." *Brain* 106, 623–642.

Libet, B. 1985. "Unconscious cerebral initiative and the role of conscious will in voluntary action." *Behav. & Brain Sci.* 8, 529–566.

Libet, B., Freeman, A., Sutherland, K. eds. 1999. "The volitional brain. Towards a neuroscience of free will." Thovrenton UK: Imprint Academic.

Lindworski, J. 1923. "Der Wille." Leipzig: Barth.
London, E.D., Ernst, M., Grant, S., Bonson, K., Weinstein, A. 2000. "Orbitofrontal cortex and human drug abuse: functional imaging." *Cerebral Cortex* 10, 334–342.
Lordkipanidze, D. et al. 2005. "The earliest toothless hominin skull." *Nature* 434, 717–718.
Lovejoy, D.W., Ball, J.D., Keats, M. et al. 1999. "Neuropsychological performance of adults with attention deficit hyperactivity disorder, ADHD, diagnostic classification estimates for measures of frontal lobe/executive functioning." *J. Internat. Neuropsychol. Soc.* 5, 222–233.
Löwith, K. 1953. "Weltgeschichte und Heilsgeschehen." Stuttgart: Kohlhammer.
Maimon, S. 1792 In: Karl Philipp Moritz' *Magazin zur Erfahrungsseelenkunde*. Vol. 9. S. 9. Berlin: Mylius.
MacKay, D.M. 1973. "The logical indeterminateness of human choices." *Brit. J. Phil. Sci.* 24, 405–408.
Malberg, J.E. 2004. "Implications of adult hippocampal neurogenesis in antidepressant action." *Rev. Psychiat. Neurosci.* 29. 196–205.
Mäkinen, I.H. 2000. "Eastern European transition and suicide mortality." *Soc. Sci. and Med.* 51, 1405–1420.
Malloy, P.F., Richardson, E.D. 1994. "Assessment of frontal lobe functions." *J. Neuropsychiat. & Clin. Neurosci.* 6, 399–410.
Manetti, G. 1532. "De dignitate et excellentia hominis." Basel. Deutsch: Über Würde und Erhabenheit des Menschen. Hamburg, Meiner 1990, Philos. Bibl. 426.
Mangels, J.A. 1997. "Strategic processing and memory for temporal order in patients with frontal lobe lesions." *Neuropsychology* 11. 207–211.
Markowitsch, H-J. 2002. "Dem Gedächtnis auf der Spur. Vom Erinnern und Vergessen." Darmstadt: Wiss. Buchgesellschaft.
Mataro, M., Jurado, M.A., Garcia-Sanchez, C. et al. 2001. "Long-term effects of bilateral frontal brain lesion: 60 years after injury with an iron bar." *Arch. Neurol.* 58, 1139–1142.
Matthey, A. 1816. "Nouvelles recherches sur les maladies de l'esprit précédées de considérations sur les difficultés de l'art de guérir." Paris: J. J. Paschoud.
Meck, W.H., Benson, A.M. 2002. "Dissecting the brains internal clock: how frontostriatal circuitry keeps time and shifts attention." *Brain & Cognition* 48. 195–211.
Mega, M.S., Cummings, J.L. 1994. "Frontal subcortical circuits and neuropsychiatric disorders." *J. Neuropsychiat. & Clin. Neurosci.* 6, 358–370.
Mick, E., Biederman, J., Faraone, S.V., Sayer, J., Kleinman, S. 2002. "Case-control study of attention-deficit hyperactivity disorder and maternal smoking, alcohol use, and drug use during pregnancy." *J. Amer. acad. child adolesc. psychiat.* 41, 378–385.
Miller, E.K. 2000. "The prefrontal cortex and cognitive control." *Nature Rev. Neurosci.* 1, 59–65.
Milner, B. 1964. "Some effects of frontal lobectomy in man." In: Akert, K., Warren, J.M. eds.: The frontal granular cortex and behavior. New York: McGraw Hill. 313–334.
Milner, B. 1982. "Some cognitive effects of frontal-lobe lesions." *Trans. R. Soc. London* B 298, 211–226.
Milner, B., Petrides, M. 1984. "Behavioural effects of frontal lobe lesions in man." *Trends neurosci.* 7, 403–407.

Mitscherlich, A. zitiert nach S. Haddenbrock. 1972. Strafrechtliche Handlungsfähigkeit und "Schuldfähigkeit," Verantwortlichkeit. In: Göppinger, H., Witter H. eds. *Handbuch der forensischen Psychiatrie* II. Berlin Heidelberg: Springer. S.885.

Miyake, A., Freidman, N.P., Emerson, M.J., Witzki, A.H., Howerter, A., Wagner, T.D. 2000. "The unity and diversity of executive functions and their contributions to complex 'frontal lobe' tasks: a latent variable analysis." *Cognit. Psychol.* 41, 49–100.

Molina, B.S., Bukstein, O.G., Lynch, K.G. 2002. "Attention-deficit/ hyperactivity disorder symptomatology in adolescents with alcohol use disorder." *Psychol. addictive behav.* 16, 161–164.

Moll, J., de Oliveira-Souza, R., Moll, F.T., Bramati, I.E., Andreiuolo, P.A. 2002. "The cerebral correlates of set-shifting: an fMRI study of the trail making test." *Arquiv. Neuro-Psiquat.* 60, 900–905.

Montesquieu, C.L. 1748. "De l'esprit des lois." Geneva.

Morrison, A., Resnik, S., Corrada, M., Zonderman A., Kawas, C. 1996. "A prospective study of estrogen replacement therapy and the risk of developing Alzheimer's disease in the Baltimore longitudinal study of aging." *Neurology* 46, suppl. 2, 435–436.

Motive zu dem Entwurf eines Bürgerlichen Gesetzbuches für das Deutsche Reich. 1888. *Amtliche Ausgabe,* Vol. I. Berlin: Guttentag, cited after Brezinka.

Mountcastle, V.B. 1957. "Modality and topographic properties of single neurons of cat's somatic sensory cortex." *J. Neurophysiol.* 20, 408–434.

Mountcastle, V.B. 1998. "Perceptual Neuroscience. The cerebral cortex." Cambridge Mass. & London, England: Harvard University Press.

Mutius, A. von ed. 1992. "Lorenz von Stein." Heidelberg: Deckers Verlag.

Namekawa, M., Fujii, T., Nishizawa, M., Nakano, I. 1999. "A case of abulia without memory disturbance due to infarction of the bilateral genua of the internal capsules." Rinsho Shinkeigaku – *Clinical Neurology* 39, 767–770.

Nauta, W.J.H. 1971. "The problem of the frontal lobe: a reinterpretaion." *J. Psychiat. Res.* 8, 167–187.

Newton, I. 1733. "Observations on the prophecies of Daniel and the apocalypse of St. John." London.

Nida-Rümelin, J. 2005. "Über menschliche Freiheit." Stuttgart, Reclam.

Nietzsche, F. 1880. „Nachlass der Achtziger Jahre." In: Schlechta ed.: Werke III, 542.

Noelle-Neumann, E. 1980. "Die Schweigespirale. Öffentliche Meinung: unsere soziale Haut." Munich: Piper.

Noelle-Neumann, E. 1997. "Wie die Skala Persönlichkeitsstärke entdeckt wurde." In: Allensbacher Jahrbuch der Demoskopie. Vol. 10. 1993–1997. Munich: Saur. 74–80.

Norman, D.A., Shallice, T. 1986. "Attention to action." In: Davidson, J.R. Schwartz, G.E., Shapiro, D. eds.: *Consciousness and selfregulation.* New York: Plenum Press. 1–18.

Norman, D.A., Shallice, T. 2000. "Attention to action: willed and automatic control of behaviour." In: M. Gazzaniga, Ed., Cognitive Neurocience. Wiley & Blackwell, pp. 376–390.

Numan, M. 1994. "A neural circuitry analysis of maternal behavior in the rat." *Acta pediat. Suppl.* 379. 19–28.

Okuda, J., Fujii, T., Yamadori, A., Kawashima, R., Tsukiura, T., Fukatsu, R., Suzuki, K, Ito, M., Fukuda, H. 1998. "Participation of the prefrontal cortices in prospective memory: evidence from a PET study in humans." *Neurosci. Lett.* 253, 127–130.

Olivi, P.J., 1248–1298. "Franziskanertheologe in Monpellier." s. *Stadter*.
O'Malley, K.D., Nanson, J. 2002. "Clinical implications of a link between fetal alcohol spectrum disorder and attention-deficit hyperactivity disorder." *Canad. J. psychiat.* 47, 349–354.
Owen, A.M., Morris, R.G., Sahakian, B.J., Polkey, C.E., Robbins, T.W. 1996. "Double dissociations of memory and executive functions in working memory tasks following frontal lobe excisions, temporal lobe excisions or amygdalo-hippocampectomy in man." *Brain* 119, 1597–1615.
Panaitios von Rhodos. 185–109 BC. Begründer der mittleren Stoa. s. *Pohlenz*.
Paganini-Hill, A., Henderson, V.W. 1994. "Estrogen deficiency and risk of Alzheimer's disease in women." *Am. J. Epidemiol.* 140, 256–261.
Pandya, D.N., Yeterian, E.H. 1990. "Prefrontal cortex in relation to other cortical areas in rhesus monkey: Architecture and connections." In: Uylings, H.B.M. et al. eds.: The prefrontal cortex. Amsterdam, New York, Oxford: Elsevier. 63–94.
Pate, R.R., Pratt, M., Blair, St.N. et al. 1995. "Physical activity and public health. A recommendation from the centers for disease control and prevention and the American college of sports medicine." *J.A.M.A.* 273, 402–407.
Petrides, M. 1996. "Specialized systems for the processing of mnemonic information within the primate frontal cortex." *Phil. Trans. Roy. Soc., Lond. Biol. Sci.* 351, 1455–1462.
Petrides, M. 1997. "Visuo-motor conditional associative learning after frontal and temporal lesions in the human brain." *Neuropsychologia* 35, 989–997.
Petrides, M., Pandya, D.N. 2002. "Association pathways of the prefrontal cortex and functional observations." In: Stuss, D.T., Knight, R.T. eds.: Principles of frontal lobe function. New York: Oxford. 32–50.
Pico della Mirandola, G. 1496. "De hominis dignitate." Über die Würde des Menschen. 1990. Philos. Bibl. 427, Hamburg: Meiner.
Planck, M. 1949. "Kausalgesetz und Willensfreiheit. Und: Vom Wesen der Willensfreiheit." In: Vorträge und Erinnerungen. 5th Edition. Stuttgart: Hirzel.
Platon, 427–347 BC "Gorgias, Symposion, Teaitet, Politeia., Nomoi, Siebenter Brief."
Pohlenz, M. 1992. "Die Stoa." 7th Edition. Göttingen: Vandenhoeck & Rupprecht.
Poldrack, R.A., Gabrieli, J-D.E. 1997. "Functional anatomy of long term memory." *J. Clin. Neurophysiol., Neurophysiol. Memory* 14, 294–310.
Popper, K.R. & Eccles J.C. 1977. "The self and its brain." Berlin, New York, London: Springer International.
Posner, M.I., Petersen, S.E. 1990. "The attention system of the human brain." *Ann. Rev. Neurosci.* 13, 25–42.
Powell, T.P.S. & Mountcastle, V.B. 1959. "Some aspects of functional organisation of the cortex of the postcentral gyrus of the monkey: a correlation of findings obtained in a single unit analysis with cytoarchitecture." *Bull. Johns Hopkins Hosp.* 105, 133–162.
Prather, M.D., Lavenex, P., Mauldin-Jourdain, M.L., Mason, W.A., Capitanio, J.P., Mendoza, S.P., Amaral, D.G. 2001. "Increased social fear and decreased fear of objects in Monkeys with neonatal amygdala lesions." *Neuroscience* 106, 653–658.
Price, C.J., Waburton, E.A., Moore, C.J. et al. 2001. "Dynamic diaschisis: anatomically remote and context-sensitive human brain lesions." *J. cognit. neurosci.* 13, 419–429.

Quiring, R., Walldorf, U., Kloter, U., Gehring, W.J. 1994. "Homology of the eyeless gene of Drosophila to the small eye gene in mice and Aniridia in humans." *Science* 265, 785–789.

Raiffeisen, F.W. 1866. "Die Darlehenskassen – Vereine als Mittel zur Abhilfe der Noth der ländlichen Bevölkerung sowie auch der städtischen Handwerker und Arbeiter." Neuwied: Strüder.

Rawls, J. 1957. "Justice as fairness." *Journ. Philosophy* 54: 653–662.

Regard, M. 1991. "The perception and control of emotion: Hemispheric differences and the role of the frontal lobes." Habilitationsschrift. Zürich.

Regard, M., Landis, T. 1997. "Gourmand syndrome. Eating passion associated with right anterior lesions." *Neurology* 48, 1185–1190.

Regard, M. Strauss, E., Knapp, P. 1982. "Childrens production on verbal and non-verbal fluency tasks." *Perceptual and motor skills* 55, 839–844.

Reiner, H. 1949. "Das Prinzip von Gut und Böse." Freiburg: Alber.

Reiner, H. 1964. "Der Sinn unseres Daseins." Tübingen: Niemeyer.

Reischies, F.M. 2005. "Psychopathologie." In: Förstl, H. ed.: *Frontalhirn. Funktionen und Grundlagen.* 2nd Edition. Heidelberg: Springer Medizin Verlag. 83–102.

Rektor, I., Kubova, D., Bares, M. 2001. "Movement-related potentials in the basal ganglia: an SEEG readiness potential study." *Clin. Neurophysiol.* 112, 2146–2153.

Rektor, I. 2003. "Intracerebral recordings of Bereitschaftspotential and related potentials in cortical and subcortical structures in human subjects." In M. Jahanshahi, M. Hallett (Eds) *The Bereitschaftspotential, movement-related cortical potentials.* Kluwer Academic / Plenum Publishers ISBN 0-306-47407-7.

Revel, J.-F. 1990. "Die Herrschaft der Lüge." Wien: Zsolnay.

Rhee, S.H., Waldmann, D. 2002. "Genetic and environmental influences on antisocial behavior." *Psychol. Bull.* 128, 490–529.

Rohracher, H. 1932. "Theorie des Willens auf experimenteller Grundlage." Leipzig: Barth.

Rolls, E.T. 1983. "The initiation of movements." In: Massion, J., Paillard, J., Schultz, W., Wiesendanger, M. eds.: *Neural coding of motor performance. Exp. Brain Res. Suppl.* 7, 24.

Rolls, E.T. 1999. "The brain and emotion." Oxford: University Press.

Rolls, E.T. 2000. "Memory systems in the brain." *Ann. Rev. Psychol.* 51, 599–630.

Rolls, E.T. 2002. "The functions of the orbitofrontal cortex." In: Stuss, D.T., Knight, R.T. eds.: *Principles of frontal lobe function.* New York: Oxford. 354–375.

Roth, G. 2001. "Fühlen, Denken, Handeln. Wie das Gehirn unser Verhalten steuert." Frankfurt: Suhrkamp.

Roth, G. 2008. "Mit Bauch und Hirn." *Die Zeit* Nr. 48. 20.11.08.

Rowland, A.S., Lesesne, C.A., Abramowitz, A.J. 2002. "The epidemiology of attention-deficit/hyperactivity disorder, ADHD, a public health view." *Ment. Retard. Developm. Disabil. Res. Rev.* 8, 162–170.

Royall, D.R., Lauterbach, E.C., Cummings, J.L., Reeve, A., Rummans, T.A., Kaufer, D.I., LaFrance, W.C. jr., Coffey, C.E. 2002. "Executive control function: a review of its promise and challenges for clinical research." *A report from the committee on*

Research of the American Neuropsychiatric Association. J.Neuropsychiat. & Clin. Neurosci. 14, 377–405.
Rushton, J.P. 2004. "Genetic and environmental contributions to pro-social attitudes: a twin study of social responsibility." *Proc. R. Lond. B Soc.* 2941, 2583–2585.
Rylander, G. 1939. "Personality changes after operations on the frontal lobes." A clinical study of 32 cases. *Acta Psychiat. Scand. Suppl.* 20, 1–327.
Sabbagh, M.A., Moulson, M.C., Harkness, K.L. 2004. "Neural correlates of mental state decoding in human adults: an event-related potential study." *J. Cognit. Neurosci.* 16, 415–426.
Scepkowski, L.A., Cronin-Golomb, A. 2003. "The alien hand: cases, categorizations, and anatomical correlates." *Behav. Cognit. Neurosci. Rev.* 2, 261–277.
Scheler, M. 1928. "Die Stellung des Menschen im Kosmos." Darmstadt: Reichl.
Schelling, F.W.J. 1808. "Philosophische Untersuchung über das Wesen der menschlichen Freiheit." In: Sämtl. Werke, 1856/7, I/7, 350.
Schmidt, W.J. 2000. "Glutamatergic mechanisms in addiction." *Neurol. Psychiat. Brain Res.* 8, 75–80.
Schneider, K. 1966. *Klinische Psychopathologie.* 7th Edition. Stuttgart: Thieme.
Schnider, A. 2001. "Spontaneous confabulation, reality monitoring, and the limbic system—a review." *Brain Res. Rev.* 36, 150–160.
Schopenhauer, A. 1819. "Die Welt als Wille und Vorstellung." § 60. Sämtl. Werke, Vol. 3 Leipzig: Brockhaus.
Schopenhauer, A. 1840. "Über die Freiheit des menschlichen Willen." In: Sämtl. Werke, Leipzig: Brockhaus. 1937.
Schore, A.N. 2000. "Attachment and the regulation of the right brain." Attachment & human developement 2, 23–47.
Schweitzer, A. 1931. "Aus meinem Leben und Denken." Hamburg: Meiner.
Schweitzer, A. 1969. "Kultur und Ethik." Munich: Beck.
Schweitzer, I., Tuckwell, V., Ames, D., O'Brien, J. 2001. "Structural neuroimaging studies in late life depression: a review." *World J. Biol. Psychiat.* 2, 83–88.
Scott, S.K., Young, A.W., Calder, A.J., Hellawell, D.J., Aggleton, J.P., Johnson, M. 1997. "Impaired auditory recognition of fear and anger following bilateral amygdala lesions." *Nature* 385, 254–257.
Seebass, G. 1993. "Freiheit und Determinismus." Z. f. philosoph. Forsch. 47, 223–245.
Seebass, G. 2007. "Willensfreiheit und Determinismus." Berlin, Akademieverlag.
Shallice, T. 1982 "Specific impairments of planning." *Phil. Trans. Roy. Soc. Lond.*, Biol. 298. 199–209.
Shallice, T. 2002. "Fractionation of the supervisionary system." In: Stuss, D.T., Knight, R.T. eds.: *Principles of frontal lobe function.* New York: Oxford. 261–277.
Shallice, T., Burgess, P. 1991. "Higher-order cognitive impairments and frontal lobe lesions in man." In: Levin, H.S., Eisenberg, H.M., Benton, A.L. eds.: *Frontal lobe function and dysfunction.* New York, Oxford: Oxford University Press, 125–138.
Shapiro, K.A., Pascual-Leone A., Motthagy, F.M., Gangitano, M., Caramazza, A. 2001. "Grammatical distinctions in the left frontal cortex." *J. cognitive neurosci.* 13, 713–720.

Shkolnikov, V.M., Field, M.G., Andreev, E.M. 2001. "Russia: Socioeconomic dimensions of the gender gap in mortality." In: Evans, T. ed.: *Challenging inequalities in death—from ethics to action.* New York, Oxford: University Press. 138–155.

Simon, H. 1927. 1929. "Aktive Krankenbehandlung in der Irrenanstalt." *Allg. Z. Psychiat.* 87, 97–145. 90, 69–121 und 245–309.

Singer, W. 2002. "Vom Gehirn zum Bewusstsein." In: *Der Beobachter im Gehirn.* Frankfurt: Suhrkamp. 60–76.

Singer, W. 2003. *Ein neues Menschenbild.* Frankfurt: Suhrkamp.

Singer, W. 2003. "Unser Wille kann nicht frei sein." Hamburg: *Spiegel spezial* 4. 20–25.

Singer, W. 2004. "Verschaltungen legen uns fest. Wir sollten aufhören, von Freiheit zu sprechen." In: C. Geyer ed. *Hirnforschung und Willensfreiheit.* Frankfurt a. M., Suhrkamp, pp. 30–65.

Sokrates, about 430 BC, see *Platon*: Phaidon, also *Xenophon*: Erinnerungen.

Solon, about 640–560 BC, see Jaspers.

Solschenyzin, A. 1974. "Der Archipel Gulag." Bern: Scherz.

Soon, C.S., Brass, M., Heinze, H.J., Haynes, J.D. 2008. "Unconscious determinants of free decisions in the human brain." Nature Neurosci. 11: 543–545.

Sophokles, about 433 BC. "Antigone." Anfang, Chor.

Spatt, J., Goldenberg, G. 1993. "Components of random generation by normal subjects and patients with dysexecutive syndroma." *Brain & cognition* 23, 231–242.

Spatz, H. 1951. "Menschwerdung und Gehirnentwicklung." Nachrichten der Giessener Hochschulgesellschaft 20: 32–55.

Sperry, R.W. 1974. "Lateral specialisation in the surgically separated hemispheres." In: Schmitt, O., Worden, F.G. eds.: *The Neurosciences. Third study program.* Cambridge, Mass.: MIT Press. 5–19.

Spinoza, B. 1677. "Ethica ordine geometrico demonstrata." Dt.: Ethik. Philosoph. Bibl. 92. Hamburg: Meiner.

Spranger, E. 1924. *Psychologie des Jugendalters.* Heidelberg: Quelle & Meyer.

Stadter, E. 1971. *Psychologie und Metaphysik der menschlichen Freiheit.* Munich, Paderborn, Wien: Verlag Ferdinand Schöningh.

Stein, H.F.K. Baron. vom & zum. 1929. *Ausgewählte Schriften.* Jena: Fischer.

Stein, L. von. 1815–1890. s. Mutius, A. von.

Steinbuch, K. 1965. "Automat und Mensch." 3rd Edition. Heidelberg: Springer.

Stephan, H., Baron, G., Frahm, H.D. 1988. "Comparative size of brains and brain components." *Neurosciences* 4, 1–38.

Stuss, D.T. 1992. "Biological and psychological development of executive functions." *Brain & Cognition* 20, 8–23.

Stuss, D.T., Alexander, M.P., Floden, D. et al. 2002. "Fractionation and localisation of distinct frontal lobe processes: Evidence from focal lesions in humans." In: Stuss, D.T., Knight, R.T. eds.: *Principles of frontal lobe function.* New York: Oxford. 392–407.

Stuss, D.T., Benson, D.F. 1984. "Neuropsychological studies of the frontal lobes." *Psychol. Bull.* Vol. 95, 1, 3–28.

Stuss, D.T., Benson, D.F. 1986. *The frontal lobes.* New York: Raven.

Stuss, D.T., Toth, I.P., Franchi, D., Alexander, M.P., Tippers, S., Craik, F.I. 1999. "Dissociation of attentional processes in patients with focal frontal and posterior lesions." *Neuropsychologia* 37, 1005–1027.

Süllwold, L. 1977. "Verhaltenstherapie an Hand von klinischen Fällen." In: Zeier, H. ed.: *Die Psychologie des 20. Jahrhunderts.* Bd. 4, 713–763. Zürich: Kindler.
Swanson, L.W., Petrovich, G.D. 1998. "What is the amygdala?" *Trends in Neurosci.* 21, 323–331.
Tang, M.X., Jacobs, D., Stern, Y. et al. 1996. "Effects of estrogen during menopause on risk and age at onset of Alzheimer's disease." *Lancet* 348, 429–432.
Tapert, S.F., Baratta, M.V., Abrantes, A.M., Brown, S.A. 2002. "Attention dysfunction predicts substance involvement in community youths." *J. Amer. Acad. Child Adolesc. Psychiat.* 41, 680–686.
Tatemichi, T.K., Desmond, D.W., Prohovnik, I. 1995. "Strategic infarcts in vascular dementia: a clinical and brain imaging experience." *Arzneimittelforschung* 45, 371–385.
Taylor, C.B., Sallis, J.F., Needle, R. 1985. "The relationship of physical activity and exercise to mental health." *Public Health Rep.* 100. 195–201.
Teuber, H.L. 1964. "The riddle of the frontal lobe function." In: Akert, K., Warren, J.M. eds.: *The frontal granular cortex and behavior.* New York: McGraw Hill.
Thaiss, L., Petrides, M. 2003. "Source versus content memory in patients with a unilateral frontal cortex or a temporal lobe excision." *Brain* 126, 1112–1126.
Thomae, H. 1969. "Entwicklung und Prägung." In: Thomae, H. ed.: Entwicklungspsychologie. In: Lersch, Ph. u.a. eds.: *Handbuch der Psychologie.* Bd. 3, 240. Göttingen: Verl. f. Psychologie. Göttingen, Hogrefe.
Thorpe, S. J., Rolls, E.T., Maddison, S. 1983. "The orbito-frontal cortex: Neuronal activity in the behaving monkey." *Exp. Brain Res.* 49, 93–115.
Tobias, P.V. 1987. "The brain of Homo habilis. A new level of organisation in cerebral evolution." *J. Hum. Evol.* 16, 741–761.
Tönnies, F. 1887. "Gemeinschaft und Gesellschaft." Neudruck Darmstadt, Wiss. Buchges. 1979.
Uhl, F., Goldenberg, G., Lang, W., Lindinger, G., Steiner, M., Deecke, L. 1990. "Cerebral correlates of imagining colors, faces and a map—II. Negative DC-potentials." *Neuropsychologia* 28, 81–93.
Uhl, F., Franzen, P., Podreka, I., Steiner, M., Deecke, L. 1993. "Increased cerebral blood flow in inferior occipital cortex and cerebellum of early blind humans." *Neurosci. Lett.* 150, 162–164.
Uhl, F., Kretschmer, G., Lindinger, G., Goldenberg, G., Lang, W., Deecke, L. 1994. "Tactile mental imagery in sighted persons and in patients suffering from peripheral blindness early in life." *Electroenceph. Clin. Neurophysiol.* 91, 249–255.
Van der Werf, Y.D., Weerts, J.G., Jolles, J. et al. 1999. "Neuropsychological correlates of a right unilateral lacunar thalamic infarction." *J. Neurol. Neurosurg. Psychiat.* 66, 36–42.
Vecera, S.P., Rizzo, M. 2003. "Spatial attention: Normal processes and their breakdown." *Neurol. Clinics* 21, 575–607.
Vergese, J., Lipton, R.B., Katz, M.J. et al. 2003. "Leisure activities and the risk of dementia in the elderly." *N. Engl. J. Med.* 348, 2508–2516.
Verschuer, O. von. 1954. "Wirksame Faktoren im Leben des Menschen." Wiesbaden: Steiner.
Vuilleumier, P., Armony, J.L., Driver, J., Dolan, R.J. 2001. "Effects of attention and emotion on face processing in the human brain: an event-related fMRI study." *Neuron* 30, 829–841.

Wallesch, C.W. 1990. "Program generator revisited: The role of the basal ganglia in language and communication." In: Deecke, L. Eccles J.C., Mountcastle, V.B. eds.: From neuron to action. Heidelberg: Springer. 299–304.

Watson, J.B. 1913. "Psychology as a behaviorist views it." *Psychol. Rev.* 20, 158–177.

Weber, M. 1922. "Gesammelte Aufsätze zur Wissenschaftslehre." Tübingen: Mohr, Siebeck.

Welsh, M.C., Pennington, B.F., Groisser, D.B. 1991. "A normative developmental study of executive function: a window on prefrontal function in children." *Developm. Neuropsychol.* 7, 131–149.

Wheeler, M.A., Stuss, D.T., Tulving, E. 1997. "Toward a theory of episodic memory: The frontal lobes and autonoetic consciousness." *Psychol. Bull.* 121, 3, 331–354.

Wilson, R.S., de Mendes Leon, C.F., Barnes L.L. et al. 2002. "Participation in cognitively stimulating activities and risk of incident Alzheimer disease." *J. Amer. Med. Ass.* 287, 742–748.

Wilson, R.S., Bennett, D.A., Bienias, J.L. et al. 2002." Coincident AD in a population based sample of older persons." *Neurology* 59. 1910–1914.

Wise, S.P., Murray, E.A., Gerfen, C.R. 1996. "The frontal cortex-basal ganglia system in primates." *Crit. Rev. Neurobiol.* 10, 317–356.

Writing Group of the Women's Health Initiative Investigation. 2002. "Risks and benefits of estrogen plus progestine in healthy postmenopausal women: principal results from the Women's Health Initiative randomized control trial." *J. Am. Med. Ass.* 288, 321–333.

Xenophon, about 400 BC. "Erinnerungen an Sokrates." Deutsch bei Heimeran.

Yoshitake, T., Kiyohara, Y., Kato, I. et al. 1995. "Incidence and risk factors of vascular dementia and Alzheimers disease in a defined elderly Japanese population:" the Hisayma study. *Neurology* 45, 1161–1168.

Yunus, M. 2009. "Creating a world without poverty: Social business and the future of capitalism." Public Affairs pp. 320 ISBN 978-1-58648-667-9.

Zeier, H. 1981. "Gehirn und Geist." In: Wendt, H. ed.: *Der Mensch. Kindlers Enzyklopädie.* Bd. 4. Zürich: Kindler. 725–738.

Ziegler, W., Kilian, B., Deger, K. 1997. "The role of the left mesial frontal cortex in fluent speech: evidence from a case of left supplementary motor area hemorrhage." *Neuropsychologia* 35, 1197–1208.

Zola-Morgan, S., Squire, L.R., Amaral, D.G. 1989. "Lesions of the amygdala that spare adjacent cortical regions do not impair memory or exacerbate the impairment following lesions of the hippocampal formation." J. Neurosci. 9, 1922–1936.

Index

f=word also on the following page
ff=word also on the 2 following pages

aboulia, 13, 50
acetyl choline, 33
activating system, reticular, 50
activation, 23, 25, 34, 80
activity, xv, 8, 16ff, 19ff, 22f, 25, 29, 38, 44ff, 50f, 54f, 57f, 59, 61ff, 66, 74f, 77f, 80f
addiction / dependence, 11, 48, 57ff, 60, 68, 82
ADHD (attention deficit hyperactivity disorder), 54
adolescence, 27f, 55f, 59, 71, 78, 80f
adopted children, 27
adrenal, 33, 51
agnosticism, total, 73
agreeableness, 26
alcohol, 5, 11, 42, 52ff, 58ff, 75, 77, 82
alcohol syndrome, fetal, 54
alcoholism in women, 54, 82
alien hand syndrome, 38
Alzheimer's dementia, 51, 60, 62, 77
aminergic, 33, 50, 60
amygdale, 33, 46ff
amyloid, 60
anatomy, anatomical, 32, 48, 73f, 81
anxiety / anxiety disorder, 12, 48, 60

anosognosia, 61
antidepressants, 11, 39, 49, 51, 57ff
apathy, 30, 32, 50
apathy, complete, 30
apes, monkeys, chimpanzees, 2, 10, 14, 26, 29, 31, 33, 35f, 40, 47, 65
aphasia, xvi, 30, 39f
apocalypse, 9
apocalyptic, 8f
art / the arts, 1, 5, 26, 43, 47
association cortex, 37, 43, 47, 49, 65, 67
association areas / fields, 31, 33, 35, 39, 47, 67, 81
attention potential, directed, 25
attention, 9, 11, 15, 30, 32ff, 35, 37, 50, 54f, 72ff, 79f
attention deficit, 54
attention, focussing of, 30
auditory area, 36, 40, 47, 63, 67, 74
authenticity, authentic, 8f, 61, 68
authority, 61
autonomy, autonomous, 12, 46, 48, 50, 75, 81

basal ganglia, 17, 30, 32ff, 35, 38f, 72, 81

Index

basal nuclei, 33f
basis, vital, 48, 68
beauty (e.g. the ~ of nature), 45, 47
behavior, antisocial, inappropriate, 27, 78
behavioral problems, 26
behaviourism, behavioristic, 14
behavior therapy, cognitive, 39
benzodiazepine (-dependency), 51, 59
Bereitschaftspotential (key word), ix, xi, xiii, xiv, xv, 16ff, 22f, 24, 38, 70, 72, 79f
birth, 12, 51f, 54, 59, 61, 71, 82
bladder dysfunction, neurogenic, 58f
blind, blindness, cortical, 1, 44, 61, 69, 71
body / physical, 27, 50, 58, 62
bond(s), instinctive, 42, 49, 56, 66
brain (key word), passim
brain areas, 18, 44, 56
brain derived neurotrophic factor, 45
brain evolution, 2
brain function, xiii, 2, 26, 28f, 31, 73, 78f
brain hemisphere(s), 18, 20f, 28f, 35f, 43, 62, 76f
brain lesions, 29f, 37, 44, 61
brain, mode of operation (actively constructing), 66
brain research, 17, 22, 29, 74
bravery / braveness, 57, 66, 68, 75

capability of freedom, xvi, 10, 12, 74
carefulness, 55
cause, caused, 14, 20, 28, 30f, 34ff, 37ff, 40f, 47f, 51, 56ff, 59f, 63ff, 71, 76, 78
cave paintings, 1, 5, 43
cerebellum, 32, 35
challenge, xv, 12, 45, 56, 62, 71
chance, xv, 9, 28, 53, 61, 69, 74, 82
character, 8, 12, 14, 26f, 30
character of the culprit, 53
child / children, 1, 6, 10f, 27f, 40f, 44ff, 47, 49, 51ff, 54ff, 58f, 61, 63, 65, 68ff, 71f, 74, 78, 80f

childhood, early, 10, 47, 52, 55, 59, 61, 65, 71f, 78, 81
cholinergic nuclei, 33, 50
cigarette(s), 42, 54, 59, 77, 82
clearness, 31
cocaine, 15, 60
columns, cortical, 42, 73
communication, 3, 15, 27, 37, 40, 56
community, 7, 30, 42, 52f, 79
community spirit, 70
compound eye (insects' ~), 42
compulsion / compulsive, 11, 39
computer, 43, 45, 62f
concentration, 11, 34, 55, 58, 79
concept / conception (of the world), 5, 8f, 13, 27f, 62
confabulation, 37
confidence, 7, 49, 51, 53, 58
conflicts of drives, 13, 51
conformism, 52
conscience, 26, 30f, 37, 41f, 49, 52, 61, 74, 80
conscience, loss of, 30, 37
conscientiousness, 26, 80
consciousness (key word), conscious, ix, xiv, 2, 13f, 24, 26, 31f, 45, 47f, 52, 61ff, 64, 68f, 71ff, 74f, 82
contingency naming test, 36
control, xiv, 3, 26, 34, 37f, 40, 42, 45, 47f, 58f, 66, 68, 71ff, 75, 80
control, emotional, 26, 80
control, self-~, xv, 5f, 11, 26f, 55f, 66, 70, 75
convexity (of cerebral [frontal] cortex), 18, 30ff, 33, 35, 80
conviction(s), 30, 33, 41, 52, 56
cooperation, xiv, 2, 9ff, 12, 18, 28f, 32, 34, 37, 39ff, 42, 44, 48f, 52f, 55f, 58f, 62f, 65, 69f, 72ff, 76, 79ff
corruption, 70
corruption, self-~, xiv, 51, 53, 79
cortex, xiii, 14, 16ff, 19, 22, 30ff, 33ff, 36ff, 39f, 43f, 47ff, 50, 53f, 58, 61ff, 65, 67, 69, 72ff, 76, 80f
cortex of will (prefrontal cortex), 18, 31f, 33ff, 36f, 43, 47f, 53f, 61, 73f, 80f

cortical blindness, 61
creative enthusiasm, 44
creativeness, 1f, 6f, 10ff, 28, 40f, 43, 45, 64, 66, 72, 81
creative strength, 28
cretinism, xvi, 75
criminality, criminal activity; ~ acts, 37, 53f, 59, 71
criminal law, 53
criminal responsibility, 53
cultural being, 1, 41
culture I, 1ff, 5, 10f, 15, 26, 41, 43, 47f, 52, 55, 65, 76, 79, 81
cybernetics, xvi, 26, 74

decision, xi, xiv, 2, 6, 9f, 24, 31, 47, 55, 72f, 74, 79
decision-making, 10, 24
decision, power/strength of, 2, 55
defects, cognitive, 43, 61
deficit(s), 54, 74
delayed response, 54
delegation of tasks (key word), xv, 18, 33
dementia, xvi, 51, 54, 57ff, 60, 62, 77f, 82
democracy, 6, 52, 69
dependence. *See* addiction
depression, xvi, 11, 13, 29, 33, 47, 49, 51, 57f, 60, 68
depressive people / persons / patients, 49, 57
depth, profoundness, 29, 31f, 47, 54f 75, 79
determinism, xi, xiii, xiv, 1, 7ff, 11, 18f, 27f, 34, 36, 59, 65f, 68ff, 72, 82
determinism, total, xiii, xiv, 9, 65f, 68, 70, 82
development, 2, 5, 13, 27f, 32, 42f, 44, 47, 52f, 55f, 59f, 65, 67, 71, 77, 80ff
development aid, 70
development, self-~, 28, 44f
diabetes, 54, 59f, 77f
dialogue, inner ~, 56
diet, 59
difficult age, 55

discharges, epileptic~, 48
discipline, xiii, 2, 8, 11, 13, 36, 47, 49, 66, 70, 75, 81
discipline, self-~, 2, 8, 10, 30, 41, 69f, 78
disinhibition, 30, 35, 37ff, 59
disinhibition, toxic ~, 75
disorders/disturbances of impetus, 51
disorders of metabolism, 51
disorders/disturbances of speech, 38, 43, 58
distraction / distractibility, 32, 36, 55, 79
distributed system, xiv, 31ff, 31, 38, 74, 76, 80, 82
dog(s), 11, 40
dolphin(s), 65
dopamine, 33
dream, 45, 52, 69
dream sleep, 45
dressage / drill / disciplining, 56, 72, 75
drive for collecting, 2, 37
drive(s), 1, 6, 10f, 14f, 30ff, 34, 40, 43, 45f, 48f, 51f, 74, 79f
drug(s) / substance(s), xvi, 11, 33, 51, 54, 59f, 75, 82
drug addiction, ~dependency, 51, 54, 59f, 75, 82
dualism, dualistic, 62
duty, duties, 26, 46, 53f, 66, 81
duty, sense of ~, 46
dysarthria, 35, 40

economic, 11, 28, 42, 70
economical impact, 60
education, xv, xvi, 10f, 26, 53ff, 56, 58, 61, 64, 70, 76, 78, 81
education, moral, 54
education, self~, 8, 56, 71, 81
ego, 8, 14, 26, 30
ego, strength of the ~, 26
egoism, 42
emotion, emotional, 26, 30, 32, 34, 37, 40, 43, 47f, 61, 69, 79ff
empathy, v, 45, 48
endurance, stamina, 2, 8, 11, 30, 58

106 *Index*

energy, 6, 11f, 14, 26, 29, 33, 42, 45, 51, 61f, 79, 82
enlightenment, 5, 7f, 13, 53
enthusiasm, enthusiastic, 44, 56, 75
environment, 8, 27f, 32
environmental influences shared / not shared, 27f, 80
envy, 52
epilepsy, epileptic, 48
epilepsy surgery, 48
estrogens, 50f, 77
ethics, ethos, xiv, xvi, 1, 5ff, 9, 28, 43, 46, 57, 66, 68, 74f, 82
evolution, evolutionary, 2f, 14, 32, 39ff, 42, 52, 67, 74, 81
example(s), 6, 18, 34, 41f, 50, 55ff, 60, 66, 69f, 75, 79, 81
executive functions (key word), ix, 15, 31, 70, 80
exercising, 45, 55f, 58f, 77
extraversion, 26
eye field, frontal, 35

factor analysis, 24, 26ff, 29
factor, neurotrophic, 44f, 57, 78
fairness, 8, 28, 41, 55, 79
faithfulness, 47, 78
family, 27, 37, 42, 55, 71
family-being, 52
fantasy, 18, 26, 36f, 69
fatigue, 51
fatigue syndrome, chronic, 51
feedback, 63
feeling(s), xiii, 7, 30, 37, 45ff, 49, 51, 56, 66, 68, 81
fields, magnetic, 29
fields, 29, 31, 33, 35, 39, 47, 66, 81
fields, association ~, 31. 33, 35, 39, 81
formation of the will, xv, 8, 28, 32, 36, 42, 49, 51, 55f, 69f, 72f, 81
freedom (key word), passim
freedom as capability, xvi, 10, 12, 74
freedom, inner, xiv, 13, 46
freedom of will, xv, 8ff, 11, 68, 75, 76, 82

freedom, reduced, 11
freedom, illusions of, 75
freedom, loss of, 54
free will (key word), xi, xiv, xv, 7ff, 13, 24, 53, 68
Freudism, 1, 14f, 34, 79
Freudian, 14f, 34, 46, 51, 68, 71
Freudomarxism, 15, 54
Friendship, xiii, xv, 18ff, 22f, 27, 29ff, 32ff, 35ff, 38ff
frontal brain, cortex, convexity, 7, 29, 31, 33ff, 42f, 45ff, 54, 56, 58, 60, 63f 69ff 77ff, 81, 87, 100, 102, 105, 112f
frontal brain test(s), 27, 55
frontal brain disorder, 54
frontal lobe (key word), xiii, 18f, 22f, 29ff, 32ff, 36f, 39f, 41, 43, 45, 48, 50, 56f, 71, 74
frontal lobe, function of, 30, 33
frontal pole, 36
functional pleasure, 46
functions, executive, ix, 15, 31, 70, 80

ganging up, 52
gene(s), genetic, 3, 14, 27f, 42, 52f, 57, 60, 71, 80
gene regulation, 3, 42
generated, generator, 17f, 40, 42, 45, 66
getting used to, 57
glia cells, 45
Global Marshall Plan, 70
goodwill or good will, 7, 53, 55, 57, 61, 66, 68, 75, 78f, 82
gourmand syndrome, 37
grandmother cell(s), 73
greed, 26, 52, 70
group influence / dynamics / pressure, 52f
guilt, 53
gyrus, cingulate, 30, 33f, 38, 47f, 80

handicap(s), handicapped, 1, 42, 82
happiness (*see also* meaning-happiness), v, 24, 45ff, 48, 56, 66, 79, 81
health, 5, 13, 50, 53, 61, 75, 77f, 82

Index

heart attack, 77
hedonism, 6, 15, 51f, 54, 66, 68, 77ff
help, xvi, 2, 12, 17, 26, 28ff, 32ff, 36, 38f, 42, 49, 51ff, 56ff, 59ff, 68, 74, 76, 78f, 81
helpful, helpfulness, 26, 48, 51
heroin, 59f, 75
hippocampal lesions, 47
hippocampus, 31f, 48, 57
histrionic(s), 49, 66
Homo erectus, 42f
Homo habilis, 40, 81
Homo sapiens neandertalensis, 43
Homo sapiens sapiens, 40, 43, 81
homocysteine, 60
honesty, 6, 28
humanized, 47, 49
humanized limbic system (emotions), 47, 79
humanity (key word), ix, 5, 47, 53, 70, 79
humanity, high ~, 47
hunger, 11f, 14, 46, 48
hyperactivity syndrome, 54
hypertension, arterial, xvi, 11, 59
hypocrisy, 52
hypothalamus, hypothalamic, 11, 30, 34, 47f, 50, 74, 81

imagination, willed ~, 18, 23, 26, 62
imagery, 80
immune defence, 50
immune system, 50, 58
impetus, 6, 22, 30, 50f
imprinting, 12, 71
impulse, 5, 13, 17, 24, 28, 30, 38, 45, 48, 68ff
independence, independent, 15, 42, 46, 52, 61f, 68, 73, 78
individual, individuality, 2, 27f, 34, 69, 80
individuum-specific, 27
infant(s), 2, 10, 45, 54, 56, 68
infection / inflammation, 51, 58f
information, 10ff 22f, 30ff, 33, 35, 38, 42, 48, 60f, 72ff

information processing, 10, 61, 63, 66, 73, 76, 82
information, compression of, 72
initiated, self-~, 2, 17f, 23, 25, 38, 56
initiation (of actions), initiated, xiii, 17f, 23, 25f, 45f, 81
initiative(s), 2, 33, 38, 70, 79
inner world, 33, 74, 80
instinct(s), 41f, 48f, 52, 66
intelligence, intelligent, 2, 26f, 29, 31, 40, 44, 52ff, 55, 65, 81
intention (key word), xiv, xv, 30, 34, 39, 53, 70
interested, interest(s), xi, xv, 24, 32, 42, 70, 79, 81
interests, mental, 2, 5
introspection, 14

Janus head (of freedom), 66
job creation, 53
joy (of children playing), 26, 46, 77

kindness, 8, 28, 66
knowledge, 1f, 5ff, 9, 11f 15, 30, 32, 63, 65, 68, 71, 73, 79

lability / instability, emotional, 37
lack of freedom (of the will), 66, 68, 72ff
law, 1, 5f, 8, 11, 53, 65, 70, 79, 82
leadership, self- ~, 1, 36, 56, 74, 79, 82
leadership (of the frontal brain, of the will), 3, 10, 15, 18, 30, 33, 41, 42, 51, 61, 70, 73f, 79f, 82
learning, xv, 10, 18ff, 21, 33, 36, 45, 52, 55f, 63, 65f, 71, 77, 79ff, 82
learning ability, 71
lesion(s) xiii, 29ff, 35ff, 38f, 43f 46f, 61, 73ff
lobotomy, 30
logos, 6
logotherapy, 57
love, 49, 54f, 57, 60
L-tryptophane, 51
lie(s), 42, 66, 70, 75

magnetic field(s) of the brain, 18, 29, 34, 73
magnetic resonance imaging, 29, 72, 74, 80
management, 2f, 34, 58f, 74, 76
management, self-~, xiv
mankind, 5, 7, 40, 42, 74, 78
Marxism, 9, 15, 54
master control genes, 3, 42
meaning-happiness (the inner happiness about the meaning of one's life), 46, 56, 66, 79
melatonin, 50
memory, passim
memory, declarative, 32
memory, episodic 37, 74
memory, long term ~, 32f, 48
memory-loss, 31, 48
memory, short time ~, 31
metarepresentation, ~-analysis, 10, 27, 73
microangiopathy, 57, 60, 77
mind, mental, 6f, 12, 14, 23, 32f, 40, 47, 49, 55, 61f, 66, 68f, 75, 79ff
mind (and brain), 12
mind, theory of ~, 45, 48
model of the brain, distributed, xiv, 31f, 33, 38, 74, 76, 80, 82
model of the brain, hierarchical, xiii, 74
mood(s), 29, 33, 50, 57
moral(s), 8, 27, 30, 32, 38, 41, 43, 54f, 57f, 66, 75, 81
mother(s), 49f, 54, 58, 71
mothers, schizophrenic, 53
motivation (key word), 24, 48, 57, 81
motor (motor functions, system), xiii, 18, 25, 27, 33, 35f, 38, 43, 63, 65, 67, 76, 81
motor area, cortex, xiii, 16f, 33, 35, 38ff, 72
movement, xiii, xiv, 14, 16ff, 19f, 22, 24f, 30, 35, 38f, 42, 45, 72f, 79f
multiple sclerosis, 31, 58
mutism (akinetic), 38

nature, natural, xvi, 3, 5ff, 8ff, 11ff, 14, 21f, 27ff, 30f, 33f, 41, 43, 47, 52, 57, 61, 66, 68f, 75f, 82
natural science, 5, 68
Neanderthal man, 43, 81
needs, internal ~, 48, 73f, 80
nervous system (vegetative), 44, 51
nerve cells, 29, 45, 57, 65, 73, 76
neuroleptics, 39, 59
neurophysiology, xv, xvi, 13, 22, 24, 39, 68f, 73f
neuroticism, neurotic, 26, 51
nobility, humane, 61, 82
noradrenaline, 33
nuclei, aminergic, 33
nuclei, cholinergic, 33, 50
nursing fees, 60
nutrition, 77, 81

obligation, 65
openness, 2, 26, 68
orbital (~ cortex), 30, 32f, 62, 80
orbital brain lesion(s), 37
orientation towards the future, willed, 57
OSCE (Organization for Security and Co-operation in Europe), 70
overweight, 59
oxytocin, 51

parallel processing, 10, 63, 73
Parkinson's disease, 17
perception, perceiving, 2, 6, 18, 23, 27, 30, 34, 42, 47, 52, 55, 61ff, 65f, 68f, 73f, 76
performance, xiv, 18ff 27, 36, 55f, 71, 74
perseveration(s), perseverance(s), 30, 36, 39
personality, 1, 10, 13, 15, 26ff, 30, 32, 37, 41ff, 47, 49, 53, 57, 61, 69, 71, 79ff, 26f, 80
personality psychology, 26f, 80
personality disorder(s), 15, 53
phobia, phobic, 57

Index

phoneme, 36, 40, 63
phylogeny, phylogenetical, 10, 34, 39, 42, 48f, 51, 62, 72f, 75f
planning, xiv, 1f, 10, 18, 24, 26, 31f, 36, 53, 56, 74f, 79f
planning, long term ~, 1, 10
planning test, 31, 36, 80
play, playing, 36, 44ff, 55, 69, 78
politics, political, 5, 11, 42, 60, 69f
powers of judgment, practical, 31
pregnancy, 54, 59, 82
prevention, xv, xvi, 26, 37, 53f, 58ff, 62, 69, 75, 77f
primates, 14, 33, 35, 40
profit, 70
prohibition, 53f
propaganda, 5, 15, 41f, 70, 75
psychiatry, 13, 15, 26, 51, 53, 59ff
psychiatry, forensic, 53
psychology, 60ff 70f, 73, 80
psychology (as discipline of the humanities), 13
psychomotor attacks, semiconscious, 48
psychosis, psychoses, 52, 59f, 82
puberty, adolescence, 43, 55
pyramidal tract, 17, 35

quantum physics, 69

reaction time, 14, 63
recall, 30, 32
recall (of intentions), 30
reflection (on oneself), self~, 6, 10, 79
rehabilitation, 58
re-learning, 45
reliability, reliable, 2, 26, 30, 32, 70
renunciation, 78
repression, 14
reprogramming, 44
research of/on will, xi, 1, 11, 15, 22, 24, 26, 79f
responsibility, responsible, xi, xiv, xv, 1f, 7f, 10f, 15, 26f, 53ff, 60, 65, 68, 71, 73ff, 79, 82

retaliation, 53
retina (of the eye), 61f, 76
reverse averaging, 16ff, 80
Rey complex figure test, 36
rhythm (circadian ~), 50
routines, unconscious~, subroutines, xiv, 26, 33, 39, 63, 72
routine processes (of the basal ganglia), 33, 72

schizophrenia, schizophrenic, 11, 51, 53, 60
sects, 59
seduced, seducers, 53, 59
selection, 2, 26, 32, 40f, 63, 72, 75, 81
self-activity, willed, 55, 57, 59
self-confidence, 7, 58
self-control, xv, 5f, 11, 26f, 55f, 66, 70, 75
self-corruption, xiv, 51, 53, 79
self-criticism, xiv, 6f, 24, 32, 37, 75
self-deception, 66, 75
self-destruction, 78
self-determination, 11, 59
self-discipline, 2, 8, 10, 30, 41, 69f, 78
self-education, 8, 56, 71, 81
self-encouragement, 56
self-esteem, 46
self-exploration, 56
self-finding, 56
self-guidance, 53
self-healing processes of the brain, 44
self-help, 58f
self-idealisation, 68
self-initiated voluntary movement, 17f, 23, 25, 38
self-initiative, 2, 56
self-leadership, 1, 36, 56, 74, 79, 82
self-liberation, 58
self-maintenance, 45
self-optimization, 44
self-organization, 6, 10, 55
self-rating scale, 31
self-realization, 28

self-regulation, xiv, 80
self-repair, 43
self-sacrifice, 75
sense of honor, 6
sense of reality (and moral will), 66
sense of responsibility, 55
sense of responsibility, social, 27
sensory, xv, 17, 22, 29, 32, 35, 40, 67, 74
sensory system(s), 54
sensory, somatosensory, 35, 39, 67, 74
separation from the mother, 71
separation of powers, 70
serotonin, 33, 39, 51
sexual behaviour, 37, 50
shame, 6f, 66
sign language, 40
sleep, the; ~, to), 11, 44f, 50f, 59
SMA (s. also supplementary motor area), 16ff, 22, 25, 38, 80f
smoking (cigarette ~), 42, 54, 59, 77, 82
social behavior, 27, 37, 40, 47, 51
social Darwinism, social Darwinists, 41
social reforms, 41
social research, 24, 26
solipsism, 58
sophronein, 6
sophrosyne, 5f
spatial, spatiality, 29, 43, 62
speech (language), xiii, 1ff, 14, 17, 27, 29f, 35f, 38ff, 40f, 43, 55, 58, 65, 72, 75, 79, 81
speech area (frontal, Broca), 35f, 39f
speech area (sensory, Wernicke's), 36, 39f
sport, 56, 58
stability, 27, 49
stamina, endurance, 2, 8, 11, 30, 58
standard(s), 43, 47, 56, 81
standard error, 21f, 25
steadfastness, 36, 42
store for programs, 33, 39
strategy, 2, 18, 31ff, 34, 36, 40, 48, 74, 78ff
streams of consciousness, 62

stress, 33, 57, 59
stress management, 59
striatum, hyperstriatum, archistriatum, 33, 48
stroke, xvi, 35, 57ff, 60, 68, 71
Stroop test, 37
sublimation, 14
subsidiarity principle, 70
suicide, 47, 60
sun, ~light, 12, 47, 57, 68
superficiality, 30
supplementary motor area (SMA), 16ff, 22, 25, 38, 72, 80f
sympathy, 48f, 69
system, distributed ~ of the brain, xiv, 31ff, 74, 76, 80, 82
system, endocrine, 47, 50
system, glutamatergic, 60
system, hierarchical ~ of the brain, xiii,13, 28, 74, 81
system, limbic (key word), ix, 30ff, 33f, 39, 45ff, 48ff, 51, 53, 60, 65, 74, 81
system, mesolimbic, 60

tactics, 18, 80
taking care, 2, 32, 41, 46, 52, 54, 81
technology, 5, 66, 75
temporal, areas, fields, lobe, 18, 23, 31ff, 36, 40, 43, 47f
term of will (naturally, reasoned), 1, 13
test(s) (frontal brain ~, etc.), 14f, 18, 27, 29, 31, 34, 36f, 43, 47, 54f, 63, 68, 71, 80
thalamus, thalamic, 31, 33, 35, 38, 50
theology, theologian, 8f
theory of mind, 48
therapy, xvi, 26, 30, 39, 57ff, 60, 62, 77
therapy by the mother, 58
therapy, behavior~, 39
therapy, psycho~, xvi, 13, 56f
thinking, thinker, thought, xi, 1f, 5ff, 8ff, 15, 18, 29ff, 32ff, 36, 41f, 45, 50, 52, 56, 59, 62, 66, 68, 73, 75, 79f, 82
thirst, 48f

thyroid gland, ~ hormones, xvi, 51, 75
tics, 39
time, xv, 6f, 11f, 15, 18, 20, 23ff, 29, 31, 38, 49, 52, 54ff, 58, 60ff, 63, 68f, 72, 74, 76, 82
time-relatedness, 62
time resolution, 29, 80
tools, 12, 43, 56
tower of Hanoi test, 31, 36, 55
tower of London test, 31, 36, 80
tragedies, 7, 78
trail making test, 36
tranquilizer, 59
trauma, 68
true, truth, 5, 7f, 14, 42, 49, 52f, 62, 66, 68, 75
twin study /studies; ~ investigation(s); ~ research, 27f, 71, 80

unconscious, the ~, xiv, 2f, 14f, 24, 52, 63, 72f, 82
understanding (incl. ~ of other people, ~ of will), 1, 9f, 15, 36f, 41, 43, 47f, 68f, 73, 77
unemployment, 59f
unreliable, unreliability, 30, 32, 68

value(s), 2, 6, 13, 15, 27f, 43, 47, 49, 56, 81
values, judgment of, 49
vanity, 52
variance (of individuality), 28
vindictiveness, 52
virtue, 6, 10, 46, 55, 57, 68
volition (key word), ix, xiii, xv, 6, 15, 18f, 23ff, 26, 35, 43 70, 80f
voluntary movements, actions, gaze etc., xiii, 17, 22, 30, 35, 38f, 70, 72, 79

wakefulness, 50, 52
weaning, 58f
Wernicke's area, ~ speech area, 36, 39f
will (key word), passim
will, cortex of (prefrontal cortex), 33, 36, 48, 81
will, disorders/dysfunctions of, 13, 31, 60
will, effort of, 14, 18, 20f, 23, 73, 80
will, formation of the ~, xv, 8, 56, 69f, 72f, 81
will for truth, 7f, 49, 62
will, freedom of, xv, 8f, 10f, 68, 75f, 82
will (individual differences), 28, 55, 81
will, paralysis of the ~, 57
will, philosophy/philosopher(s) of the ~, xiv, xv, 9f, 24, 26, 47, 53, 57
will, process of ~, states, 26, 29
will, research of/n ~, 11, 15, 17, 24, 26, 58, 79f
will, reasoned, xvi, 9, 40, 48f, 51f, 57, 70, 81
will, strength of ~ (*see also* willpower), 28, 55, 57ff
will, term of (naturally, reasoned), 1, 13
willing, the (reasonable), 8f
willpower, 7, 50, 52, 82
Wisconsin card sorting test, 27, 34, 36, 55, 71
working memory, 15, 31, 54, 59, 80

young persons / youngsters, 12, 14, 27f, 53f, 82
youth groups, 61

Zen, 58

Name Index

Ach, Narziss, 14
Alexander, Gene E., 34, 39
Allport, Gordon W., 57
Amelang, Manfred, 26
Anderson, Adam K., 36f, 47, 56
Anokhin, Pyotr, 27, 71
Anselm of Canterbury, 7, 27
Aquinas, Thomas of, 7
Aristotle, 6f, 41, 46, 57, 68
Asch, Solomon E., 52
Aschoff, Jürgen, xvi
Asenbaum, Susanne, xvi
Asendorpf, Jens B., 26f

Bartussek, Dieter, 26
Baumann, Bruno, 57
Baumgartner, Christoph, xvi
Bechinger, Doris, xvi, 44, 58, 76
Becker, Wolfgang, xvi
Beckmann, Jürgen, 24
Beisteiner, Roland, xvi
Benson, D. Frank, 34, 61f
Berkeley, George, 73
Berrios, German E., 15
Bismarck, Otto von, 41
Boden, Günther, 60
Bonaventura, 7
Boschert, Jürgen, xvi
Brezinka, Wolfgang, 54

Brunner, Richard J., 39
Bruno, Giordano, 9, 42
Bühler, Charlotte, 11, 28
Bühler, Karl, 46

Carus, Carl Gustav, 14f
Cézanne, Paul, 66
Cheyne, Douglas, xvi
Cicero, 5
Conrad, Bastian, xvi, 63
Copernicus, Nicolaus, 42
Coulmas, Florian, 75
Cramon, Yves von, 34
Creutzfeldt, Otto Detlev, xvi, 73
Crick, Francis, 45
Cui, Rong Qing, xvi
Cummings, Jeffrey L., 39, 48
Cunnington, Ross, xvi, 38
Cusanus, Nicholas (of Cusa), 7, 9, 28
Czikszentmihalyi, Mihaly, 34, 46

Darwin, Charles, 14, 41f, 70
Deci, Edward L., xiv, 24
Deecke, Lüder, xi, xiii, xiv, xv, xvi, 16f, 19, 22f, 25, 29, 38, 72, 80
Democritus, 5f, 57, 69
Dennett, Daniel C., xi, xiv, 11, 64, 69
Descartes, René, 7, 9, 62
Diekmann, Volker, xvi

Dilthey, Wilhelm, 13
Diogenes Laertius, 6
Dostojewski, Fjodor Michailowitsch, 57
Dunant, Henry, 41
Duns Scotus, Johannes (John), 7, 27, 46

Eccles, John C. (Sir), xiv, xvi, 22, 24
Eckermann, Johann Peter, 58
Endl, Walter, xvi
Engel, Marion, xvi
Erasmus of Rotterdam, 7
Erdler, Markus, xvi
Ernst, Cecil, 71
Espy, Kimberly Andrews, 55
Eysenck, Hans Jürgen, 15

Fichte, Johann Gottlieb, 8, 13
Filley, Christopher M., 26
Frankl, Viktor E., xvi, 46, 57
Franciscus of Assisi, Franciscans, 7f, 28, 42
Fratiglioni, Laura, 60
Fredrickson, John M., xvi
Freeman, Walter J., 30
Freud, Sigmund, 1, 9, 14f, 34, 45f, 51, 54, 71, 79
Fröbel, Friedrich, 57

Galilei, Galileo, 22
Gautama (Buddha), 41, 58
Gehlen, Arnold, 41
Gerschlager, Willibald, xvi
Goethe, Johann Wolfgang von, 36, 43, 46, 56, 58, 76
Goldberg, Gary, 14
Goldenberg, Georg, xvi, 23, 36
Goldin-Meadow, Susan, 40
Goldman-Rakic, Patricia S., 31, 54
Gollwitzer, Peter Max, 22, 24, 26
Goschke, Thomas, 24
Grotius, Hugo, 41
Gutenberg, Johannes, 70

Haggard, Patrick, 26
Hallett, Mark, 24

Haynes, John-Dylan s. Soon et a., 73
Hartmann, Eduard von, 15
Hartmann, Nicolai, 9f
Heckhausen, Heinz, 15, 22, 24
Hegel, Georg Friedrich Wilhelm, 8f
Heimer, Lennart, 48
Heinroth, Johann Christian August, 13
Heisenberg, Werner, 69
Held, Richard, 44f
Hellbrügge, Theodor, 61
Heracles, 6, 56
Heraclitus, 6, 14, 28, 42, 69, 74
Hershberger, Wayne A., xiv, 24
Hess, Walter Rudolf, 11
Heston, Leonard L., 53, 71
Hetzer, Hildegard, 55
Hinkle, Lawrence E., 52
Hölderlin, Friedrich, 46, 76
Hoehne, Ottomar, xvi
Horkheimer, Max, 15
Holloway, Ralph L., 40
Holst, Erich von, xvi
Howard, George S., 75
Huizinga, Johan, 9
Huckabee, Mary Lee, xvi
Hülser, Paul Jürgen, xvi
Humboldt, Alexander von, 43
Humboldt, Wilhelm von, 56

Iggo, Ainsley, xvi
Ingvar, David, 24
Iwase, Katsuhiko, xvi

Jahanshahi, Marjan, 17, 24
James, William, xiv, 13, 24
Janzarik, Werner, 53
Jaspers, Karl, xv, xvi, 8, 13, 15, 56
Jessen, Peter Willers, 61
Jesus, 6, 8f, 41, 75
Jones, Ernest, 15, 29
Jürgens, Reinhard, xvi
Jung, Richard, xvi

Kamei, Tamio, xvi
Kane, Robert, xiv, 24

Name Index

Kanfer, Frederick H., xiv, 24
Kant, Immanuel, xv, 5, 7f, 10f, 13, 28, 41, 66
Kawamura, Koki, 29
Kekulé, Friedrich August (von Stradonitz), 45
Kierkegaard, Sören, 9, 13, 56
King, Abby C., 58
Kim, Jin-Soo, xvi
Kirchbach-Henneberg, Alexandra von, xvi
Kleiser, Bernhard, xvi
Kleist, Karl, xvi, 30f, 34, 80
Knight, Robert T., 34, 48
Kohler, Ivo, 45
Kornhuber, Anselm, xvi
Kornhuber, Hans Helmut, passim
Kornhuber, Johannes, xvi
Kornhuber, Malte, xvi
Kriebel, Jürgen, xvi
Kristeva, Rumyana, xvi
Kropotkin, Fürst Pjotr Alexejewitsch, 41f
Kuhl, Julius, 24
Kungtse (Confucius), 8, 28, 41, 57, 61, 74f

Lalouschek, Wolfgang, xvi
Lang, Michael, xvi, 18ff, 21, 25
Lang, Wilfried, xvi, 18ff, 21, 23, 25, 29
Lashley, Karl S., 44, 74
Leibniz, Gottfried Wilhelm, 13f, 62
Lengfelder. Angelika, 26
Lenin, Wladimir, Iljitsch, 41
Leon, David A., 54
Lessing, Gotthold Ephraim, 42
Leubuscher, Rudolf, 13
Levin, Harvey S., 55, 58
Lewin, Kurt, 14
Libet, Benjamin, 24, 72
Lindinger, Gerald, xvi, 21
Lindworski, Johannes, 13
Löwith, Karl, 9
Luckner, Nikolaus von, 71
Luther, Martin, 7ff

MacKay, Donald M., 11
Maimon, Salomon, 13
Malloy, Paul F., 34, 37
Markowitsch, Hans, 32
Marx, Karl, 9, 15, 41, 54
Matthey, André, 13
Mauch, Erik, xvi
Mayer, Dagmar, xvi
Mega, Michael S., 48
Mill, John Stuart, 70
Milner, Brenda, 36
Mirandola, Pico della, Giovanni, 7, 28, 41, 46
Mitscherlich, Alexander, 68
Montesquieu, Charles de Secondat, Baron de, 41, 70
Moritz, Karl Philipp, 13
Moser, Ewald, xvi
Mountcastle, Vernon B., xvi, 42, 73f

Nell-Breuning, Oswald von, 70
Newton, Sir Isaac, 9, 69
Nida-Rümelin, Julian, 26
Nietzsche, Friedrich, 8, 10f, 15, 28, 46, 57
Noelle-Neumann, Elisabeth, 24, 52, 61
Norman, Donald A., 26

Okuda, Jiro, 32
Oldenkott, Bernd, xvi
Olivi, Petrus Johannis, 7, 28, 75

Panaitius of Rhodos, 5, 47
Pandya, Deepak N., 29, 32
Paulus, 8
Peckham, John, 7
Pestalozzi, Johann Heinrich, 55, 57
Petrides, Michael, 30, 32, 36
Pindar, 56
Planck, Max, 22, 24, 65
Plato, 6, 8, 13, 41, 46, 56, 62, 68, 70
Podreka, Ivo, xvi
Pohlenz, Max, 47
Popper, Karl R. (Sir), xiv, 24

Potthoff, Peter, xvi
Powell, T.P.S., 29, 42

Raiffeisen, Friedrich Wilhelm, 41
Regard, Marianne, 36f
Reiner, Hans, 6, 66
Revel, Jean-Francois, 70
Rhee, Soo Hyun, 27
Richter, Hans Peter, xvi
Riebler, Rosl, xvi
Rohracher, Hubert, 14
Roth, Gerhard, 47, 71f, 75
Royall, Donald R., 26
Rushton, J. Philippe, 27
Rutschmann, Alexandra, xvi

Scheid, Peter, xvi, 17
Schelling, Friedrich Wilhelm Joseph, 8
Schneider, Kurt, xv, xvi, 13
Schopenhauer, Arthur, 14ff, 65
Schreiber, Herbert, xvi
Schweitzer, Albert, 8f, 42f, 57
Scott, Sophie K., 47
Seebass, Gottfried, 26
Seneca, 5
Shallice, Tim, 26, 31, 34, 36, 80
Shkolnikow, Vladimir M., 54
Simon, Hermann, 59
Singer, Wolf, 73ff
Socrates, 6, 9, 13, 42, 46, 56, 75
Solon, 6, 41f
Solschenizyn, Alexander Issajewitsch, 70
Soon, Chun Siong, 73
Sophocles, 28, 41, 66
Spatt, Josef, xvi, 36
Spatz, Hugo, 42
Sperry, Roger W., 62
Spinoza, Baruch, 9, 42
Spranger, Eduard, 13
Stadter, Ernst, 7
Stalin, Joseph, 41
Starr, Arnold, xvi

Stein, Baron vom & zum, Heinrich, Friedrich, Karl, 41, 70
Stein, Lorenz von, 41
Steinbuch, Karl, xvi, 64
Stephan, Heinz, 39
Stuss, Donald T., 34, 61f
Süllwold, Lilo, 57

Taylor, C. Barr, 58
Teuber, Hans Lukas, 30
Thomae, Hans, 71
Tobias, Philipp V., 40
Tönnies, Jan Friedrich, xvi
Tönnies, Ferdinand, 42
Toqueville, Alexis de, 70
Trotzki, Leo, 41

Uhl, Frank, xvi, 18, 21, 23, 44

Verschuer, Otmar von, 28
Vrba, Jiři, xvi

Walla, Peter, xvi
Wallesch, Claus P., xvi, 39
Walter of Bruges, 7
Watson, John B., 14
Weinberg, Hal, xvi
Weinert, Franz E., 22
Welsh, Marilyn C., 55
Westphal, Klaus Peter, xvi
Wheeler, Mark A., 74
Widder, Bernhard, xvi
Wiest, Gerald, xvi
Windischberger, Christian, xvi
Wolff, Harold G., 52
Wright, Georg Henrik von, 11
Wundt, Wilhelm, 14

Xenophanes, 6
Xenophon, 6

Yunus, Muhammad, 42

Zarathustra, 5, 8, 11
Zeier, Hans, 22

www.ingramcontent.com/pod-product-compliance
Lightning Source LLC
Chambersburg PA
CBHW070643300426
44111CB00013B/2245